# THE SCHOOLBOOK PROTEST MOVEMENT

## 40 QUESTIONS & ANSWERS

by
Edward B. Jenkinson
Indiana University

Phi Delta Kappa Educational Foundation
Bloomington, Indiana

cover design by Keiko Kasza

## Dedication

To the memory of my niece, Mary Kathryn Jenkinson Dungan, who was a most inspiring young teacher —

and to the memory of my friends, Bernarr Folta, Lawrence Haddad, and Paul Jacobs — all great teachers, each in his own way.

# Acknowledgments

Nearly three years ago, Derek Burleson, editor of special publications for Phi Delta Kappa, suggested that I write this book. He has been patient, quietly persistent, and gently persuasive ever since. I am very pleased that he requested the book, and I am very relieved that it is now finished. So are my wife, Ronna, and our children, Andrea, Mark, and Nicholas. They endured during the writing, and they encouraged me after late nights and early mornings at the word processor.

Bobbi Shank, Julie Bach, and Amy Foster searched through filing cabinets and boxes filled with newspaper clippings, magazine articles, and letters, sometimes vainly attempting to find what I felt I needed at once. They, too, offered encouragement when it was needed most, as did J. Charles Park, professor of education at the University of Wisconsin — Whitewater. His kind words and his dedication to research were inspiring, as was the work of Barbara Parker of People for the American Way, who has been tireless in her efforts to protect the freedom to learn in this country.

Parts of some of the answers in this book are based on writing I did for other publications, including *Censors in the Classroom* (Southern Illinois University Press, 1979). My earlier words and ideas in these articles served as aids in writing some of the answers herein: "Protecting Holden Caulfield and His Friends from the Censors," *English Journal*, January 1985; "Schoolbook Skirmishes Leave Longlasting Scars," *The National Forum*, to be published in late 1985; "The Tale of Tell City: An Anti-Censorship Saga," a discussion paper published by People for the American Way, 1983; "The Censorship Tale of Tell City," *Indiana English*, Spring 1983; and "Is Secular Humanism Being Taught in Our Public Schools?" *Church & State*, May 1983.

I wish to thank the Madison (Wisconsin) Metropolitan School District and the Iowa Department of Public Instruction for permission to reprint their instructional materials policies, and the National Education Association for permission to reprint part of *How Fair Are Your Children's Textbooks?*

# Contents

# The First Amendment and the Schoolbook Protest Movement: A Personal Assessment

*Congress shall make no law respecting an establishment of religion, or prohibiting the free exercise thereof; or abridging the freedom of speech, or of the press; or the right of the people peaceably to assemble, and to petition the government for a redress of grievances.*

The 45 words of the First Amendment have intrigued me from the time I enrolled in an introductory journalism course as an undergraduate. Even before that I read about John Peter Zenger, the colonial printer whose trial helped to establish freedom of press in America. As a high school student, I studied some of the early writings of Benjamin Franklin, and I marveled at the courage of his editor brother who was jailed for criticizing both civic and religious leaders. And I occasionally considered the words of Thomas Jefferson in a letter to Colonel Edward Carrington: "The basis of our government being the opinion of the people, the very first object should be to keep that right; and were it left to me to decide whether we should have a government without newspapers, or newspapers without a government, I should not hesitate to prefer the latter." As I continued to study journalism and English and as I taught in junior and senior high schools, I added to my knowledge of the First Amendment, I thought; but, in reality, I knew very little.

The First Amendment, it seemed to me early in my study, was something invoked by journalists to protect a free press. It also protected free speech, but that protection was limited when it came to radio and to television in its infancy. Somehow, I learned, the First Amendment also guaranteed academic freedom; but as a high school teacher in the early Fifties, I did not worry about that. Who needed academic freedom to teach *Silas Marner* and traditional grammar?

In my first two years of teaching, I never questioned the principal's right to begin faculty meetings, PTA meetings, and some after-school functions with prayer. The Supreme Court had not yet acted on *Abington v. Schempp*, and prayer in a little country school seemed almost to be part of the curriculum. At least two of the elementary teachers started the school day with prayer.

1

But I could not say prayers aloud in my classroom — even if I had been so inclined. The township trustee had warned me when I signed my first contract that I was not to proselytize. He said that he was taking a chance on hiring the "very first Catholic" to teach in that school system. When he asked if I would try to convert the students, I dismissed his question with the response that I was there to teach English — not Catholicism. But as I participated in school functions, I learned one disquieting fact: my prayers were out, his were in.

No one's prayers should be sanctioned by the public schools. But certain prayers were recited in chorus in the Fifties in some school systems, and they still are today despite the Supreme Court's decision. The separation of church and state — a guarantee of the First Amendment — is as misunderstood today as it was when I began teaching. I knew some of my students prayed then. They did so silently during tests; they probably prayed at other times too. No one could have stopped their voluntary prayers. The same is true today. Truly *voluntary* prayer has not — nor cannot — be removed from public schools despite what the critics claim.

My students and I referred to the Bible in my English classes when it provided the basis for allusion or symbol in the literature we were reading. No one objected then. No reasonable person would object today when the Bible is studied as great literature. And it is studied as such in hundreds of schools even though some critics charge that the Bible was thrown out of public school by the Supreme Court, which is a misreading of the decision.

At least one-third of my students read two to three books a month. I encouraged them to do so. This caused the librarian in the closest small city to call me to ask what magic formula I was using to persuade students to check so many books out of the library. I simply told her that I talked about books in my classes; I got excited about books. Some of my students did also.

My interest in books nearly caused me trouble during my first two years of teaching. The minister in the small town in which the school was located did not like the fact that many of my students were reading — and discussing — not only the classics but contemporary literature. He expressed his concerns in two different sermons, calling me by name and implying that my teaching methods were dangerous. But

I was totally unaware of his concerns. No one told me about the sermons until after I moved to a large city school but continued to live in the small community. Only then did several students and their parents talk to me about the sermons. And they seemed embarrassed when they talked about them. They said they refused to tell me about the sermons before because they did not want me to stop what I was doing.

During the three years that I taught in a large junior-senior high school, I experienced no problems with complaints about what I taught or what I did in classes. The faculty rarely — if ever — discussed academic freedom and censorship. My colleagues and I were both amused and embarrassed by the Indiana senator who tried to get *Robin Hood* banned from the state because it was allegedly communistic. On one occasion several of us discussed the firing of a teacher "somewhere" for teaching *The Catcher in the Rye*; but the incident seemed far away, and problems over textbooks and other teaching materials seemed to be something that only happened "somewhere else." (That is still the case today. Teachers and administrators, when I ask about their personal involvement in censorship incidents, inevitably tell me that they "didn't think it could happen here." Censorship always happens "somewhere else.")

I left public school teaching shortly before attempts to remove school and library books intensified. The McCarthy era had left its legacy of fear. Signing a loyalty oath was standard procedure. The hunt for leftist-leaning textbooks was under way. And Holden Caulfield had captured the attention of students and teachers throughout the nation. *The Catcher in the Rye* had entered some English classrooms as a contemporary classic. Some teachers lost their jobs because of Holden's antics and language; others started teaching *The Catcher* 30 years ago and have done so ever since without incident.

Such is the nature of schoolbook protest in America. No one can predict where it will occur; no one can foretell what book will inflame citizens to the point that they will attempt to have it removed from classrooms and libraries — or even have it burned. No book is safe, I learned. Any idea is a target for someone.

But it took me years to discover that. My sojourn from the public schools took me to university public relations for two years before I went to Beirut, Lebanon, to teach journalism. Then I returned to Indiana and began a long relationship with Indiana University and with the public schools, working closely with teachers of English, speech, and journalism.

At the beginning of the Seventies, some of the teachers who had worked with me on developing courses of study for junior and senior high school English classes began calling me for help. They told me that a few parents were challenging some of the books they were teaching. Those books had been recommended in the courses of study I had edited or helped to write, and some of the books had been taught for years in the very schools in which they were suddenly being challenged. I was amazed to learn that parents did not want their children reading *The Red Badge of Courage* (too much violence), *The Scarlet Letter* (adultery), *Siddhartha* (pagan religion), and *To Kill a Mockingbird* (obscene language and disrespect for parents). I began investigating the complaints against those and other books not only in Indiana but throughout the nation. I was alternately amused and horrified.

It is difficult to take some of the complaints seriously. One woman objected to the teaching of *Silas Marner* on the grounds that she "knew what that dirty old man is doing to that little girl . . . between chapters." A school board member demanded that the librarian be fired for having *Making It with Mademoiselle* in the school library. I understand that he withdrew his request when he learned that it was a book of dress patterns. A parent complained that *Jack and the Beanstalk* teaches disrespect for a person in authority (the giant). And the two most prominent textbook protesters in the nation objected to the inclusion of P.T. Barnum's famous statement, "There's a sucker born every minute," in a story in a textbook because Barnum's philosophy is "skeptical" and the statement is "depressing."

I found it difficult to believe that people would actually object to books without having read them, or without even having checked the accuracy of the titles, or without even having talked with a teacher to determine whether a book was actually used in a classroom or to a librarian to determine whether it was in the school library. Even more difficult to believe is that a few school administrators, teachers, librarians, and school board members are willing to act on such objections without becoming familiar with the material themselves.

After two years of studying attempts to censor school materials, I was asked to serve as chairman of the Committee on Censorship of the National Council of Teachers of English (NCTE) in 1976. Shortly after accepting the chairmanship, I received several letters of congratulations on my appointment to chair a group that would rid the nation's schools of objectionable books. I urged NCTE to change the name of the group to the Committee Against Censorship so that there would be no confusion about the mission of the committee.

As chairman of the NCTE committee, I received reports of complaints about classroom and library materials across the land, including those of the prominent textbook protesters in Texas, Mel and Norma Gabler, the founders of Educational Research Analysts, which they call the world's "largest textbook review clearinghouse." It did not take me long to learn how influential they had become through using the Texas textbook adoption process (see questions 19, 20, and 21). I soon discovered that they scoured every textbook submitted for adoption in Texas, searching for anything that did not coincide with their religious and political points of view or with their conceptions of reality. I felt that if I were to understand the full range of censorship of school materials, I had to meet them. I soon had that opportunity.

Shortly after the *Chicago Tribune* published a feature story about my research, an associate producer of *The Phil Donahue Show* called to ask me why I was attempting to censor textbooks. When I told her that I was opposed to censorship, she asked why I had so many targets. When I explained that the targets published in the *Tribune* were those of the people whose objections I had been studying, she was disappointed. She indicated that the producers were looking for censors, not for college professors who studied censorship. But when she said that she might invite me to be on the program if I could name a few censors, I quickly suggested Norma and Mel Gabler.

In a letter to their followers about their invitation to be on the program, the Gablers proclaimed:

> "Censorship" in the context of this program means all parents who dare question any school program. We have been selected to represent the many parent groups who are concerned about the consistent attacks upon Judeo-Christian moral values in library and textbooks in public schools. . . .

> We CANNOT censor a book, because we're neither the authors or editors of school books, but the word "censor" is an effective smear term since most Americans are against censorship . . . .
>
> Actually, we are pointing out that censorship *has* taken place. Library and textbooks have been censored of practically everything worthwhile, joyful, moral, uplifting, constructive and beautiful . . . .
>
> IN OPPOSITION will be the chairman of the CENSORSHIP COMMITTEE of The NATIONAL COUNCIL OF TEACHERS OF ENGLISH. This organization has long been a strong proponent of the so-called "realism" which fills currently used school books. This means violence, street language, explicit sex, etc.

I prize that letter, and I refer to it frequently not only to raise my spirits but to remind me of the Gabler point of view. I also prize my experience on *Donahue*. The Gablers apparently felt that since there were two of them and only one of me, they could take two-thirds of the time, which they managed to do. Apparently, they also requested permission to have many friends in the audience who were sympathetic to their cause. The driver of the show's limousine told me as he took me back to the airport that there were "two busloads of censors" in the audience. That information caused me to smile even more when I read this paragraph from a letter the Gablers sent to their followers two days after the broadcast:

> God certainly answered prayer, so that even the studio audience ended up almost entirely on our side, while the opposition made statements which will likely prove embarrassing to them in the future.

People still talk to me about that telecast of January 1978. Nearly all who said they thought little about censorship before the telecast indicated that the program helped them see the problems that accompany attempts to remove books from school classrooms and libraries. Nearly everyone expressed an antipathy toward censorship as a result of the show.

I debated Mel Gabler four times after that: twice on radio, once on television in Chicago, and once in a formal debate during a convention of a professional organization in Houston. During that debate, I used several Gabler quotations that had been printed in *Texas Monthly*.

Among them was this one, which I think is indicative of the depth of the Gabler scholarship:

> Roman Catholics do not teach the gospel, and are, therefore, not necessarily Christians.

In his rebuttal, Mel Gabler said that the reporter had misquoted him. I waited for the actual quotation. But Mr. Gabler simply told the audience that the reporter had left out the word *all*.

Mel Gabler told a 1980 *Donahue* audience that the Gabler reviews of textbooks have been used in all 50 states and 25 foreign countries. Their influence alone is enormous; they also have powerful allies. For example, the Rev. Jerry Falwell, one of the founders of the Moral Majority, uses the Gablers' reviews of textbooks to show how bad the books are; and he described the Gablers' work in *Listen, America!* and in at least one other of his publications. The Rev. Tim LaHaye, another founder of the Moral Majority, uses the Gablers' reviews, as well as other sources, to prove that the public schools are "conduits to the minds of youth, training them to be anti-God, antimoral, antifamily, anti-free enterprise and anti-American." Phyllis Schlafly, founder of Eagle Forum and the Stop Textbook Censorship Committee, has used the Gabler reviews to attack schoolbooks throughout the nation.

In my writing and in my debates with schoolbook protesters, I constantly point out that citizens have the right to complain about the content of textbooks. As a parent, I have that right. If I do not like something that my children are reading in school, I have the right to object. But I believe that my rights as a parent extend only to my children. If I do not like what they are reading or studying, I can ask for an alternate assignment. But I maintain that my rights as a parent do not extend to all the children in the classroom, or in the school, or in the state, or in the nation.

That is one of the many differences between the schoolbook protesters and the thousands of citizens who do not want teaching materials and teaching methods removed willy-nilly from the public schools. Another major difference is that most parents I know who support the schools are unwilling to judge a book or a teacher solely on the basis of someone else's statements. But many schoolbook protesters — whether they are nationally prominent or known only locally — are willing to base their accusations on the objections of the Gablers, of Phyllis Schlafly and the Eagle Forum, of Tim LaHaye, of the Moral Majority, or on the objections of one of the hundreds of textbook protesting organizations that have been formed during the last decade.

So that I could better understand their concerns about schoolbooks and their strategies to remove them, I read reams of objections and also at least 40 books and monographs critical of public education. I also made every attempt to meet the protesters. Fortunately, many opportunities presented themselves. I discussed censorship with the Rev. Greg Dixon, then national secretary of the Moral Majority, seven times — once on the *Today Show*, once on local television, and five times in formal debates. I debated Cal Thomas, vice president of the Moral Majority, on *CBS Nightwatch*. A producer of the *MacNeil/Lehrer Report* invited me to present my views on censorship in opposition to those of Janet Egan, one of the founders of Parents of Minnesota, Inc. I also had the opportunity to be interviewed for *60 Minutes, CBS Sunday Morning, The John Davidson Show*, and more than 30 television programs in a dozen states. On a number of those programs I was given the chance to express my views in an exchange with schoolbook protesters.

Shortly after the publication of *Censors in the Classroom* in 1979, I was invited to be a guest on more than 100 radio programs in more than 30 states, Great Britain, and Canada. On at least half of those programs, which were call-in shows, I had the opportunity to exchange views with schoolbook protesters.

My study of censorship also afforded me the opportunity to talk with teachers, librarians, administrators, students, and parents in more than 30 states, including presentations on Phi Delta Kappa's Distinguished Lecture Series. In 1982 Phi Delta Kappa with Indiana University's School of Education and School of Continuing Studies conducted a national conference on the public schools and the First Amendment. That was a memorable experience for me since I was privileged to serve as co-director of the conference, which featured an equal number of schoolbook protesters and persons opposed to censorship.

As I met more and more persons concerned with the content of textbooks and library books, I became aware of their intense objection to the words *censor* and *censorship* (see questions 4 and 7). I also realized that those words did not refer to the variety of activity concerning schoolbooks, teaching materials, and teaching methods that was being promoted across the nation. Therefore, I began using the term *schoolbook protest movement* (see questions 1 and 2).

When Derek Burleson, editor of special publications for Phi Delta Kappa, asked me to write this book on the schoolbook protest movement, he suggested that I focus on the questions that I am asked most frequently as I talk with teachers, librarians, administrators, school board members, students, and parents. So I selected 40 questions to answer.

I have limited the questions and answers only to the protest of books and materials used in public schools. Although I am very much interested in attempts to censor the student press, I have not discussed such censorship here. That would require yet another book. Nor do I pose questions on, or provide answers about, pornography. No court in this land has found any book taught in the public schools to be pornographic, contrary to what some of the protesters claim. Nor has any book used in the public schools and considered by the courts been labeled obscene.

The answers to the 40 questions I pose obviously vary in length and treatment, but in each case I have tried to answer them to give as complete a picture of the schoolbook protest movement as I can. However, the movement is not static; it changes at least monthly if not more frequently. There are always new targets, new tactics, and new faces. But the basic ingredients of the movement remain the same, and I have tried to describe them here.

# Questions and Answers

## 1. What is the schoolbook protest movement?

Schoolbook protest movement is a term I have been using during the last two years to describe attempts to remove or alter teaching materials and teaching methods used in the public schools. I prefer schoolbook protest to censorship for these reasons:

1. Attempts to remove books from school classrooms and school libraries across the nation are not necessarily unrelated incidents. There is a movement, inspired and promoted by dozens of organizations, that is sweeping the country. (See questions 14, 15, 16, 17, 18, 19, 22, 23, 24, 26, and 30.)

2. Schoolbook protest encompasses the objections of individual citizens who, without consulting others, object to a single book or to books their children are studying. The term is also applicable to the work of school critics who have attempted to remove, or keep from being adopted, books and teaching methods on a nationwide or statewide scale. Such critics include Norma and Mel Gabler and their Educational Research Analysts, Phyllis Schlafly and her Eagle Forum and Stop Textbook Censorship Committee, Beverly LaHaye and her Concerned Women of America, as well as Tim LaHaye and his attacks on the religion of secular humanism and on any books or courses that he thinks promote that so-called religion. (See questions 14, 15, 16, 17, 18, 19, 22, 23, 24, and 26.)

3. Protesters dislike being called censors. They maintain that they do not have the power to remove books from schools; they only point out the problems in teaching materials and teaching methods. (See questions 4 and 7.)

4. Not all persons who protest textbooks and library books want them removed from the schools or even placed on restricted shelves. Some persons simply want to call attention to items that they do not like or to items that they think need to be counterbalanced with other material.

5. The term schoolbook protest movement, for me at least, can be applied to the actual censorship of school materials as well as to consciousness raising. (See question 7.)

6. Schoolbook protest can be applied to objections to textbooks at statewide hearings, such as those conducted in Texas, where persons attempt to prevent the textbooks from being adopted or to have them altered before they are adopted. It also can be applied to objections recorded at school board meetings. (See questions 20 and 21.)

7. Schoolbook protest encompasses actual removal of books, attempts to restrict their access, efforts to erase or remove specific words or pages, as well as prior restraint (attempts to direct the work of writers and publishers so that they will not include certain words, ideas, or actions in their books, stories, poems, and plays).

## 2. When did the schoolbook protest movement begin?

From the time that students began attending public schools in large numbers, individuals and groups have expressed displeasure with the content of textbooks. For example, immediately after the Civil War, veterans from both sides pressured publishers to change histories that they said did not reflect their reasons for fighting at Shiloh, Bull Run, and Gettysburg. "Some publishers surrendered to the demands of the veterans without firing a shot. In 1867 . . . E.J. Hale and Son of New York advertised: 'Books prepared for southern schools, by southern authors, and therefore free from matter offensive to southern people.' "[1]

"In the North, the *Grand Army Record* urged Union veterans to 'aid in dashing down the cup of moral poison that our school histories are holding to your youth.' A committee of the Grand Army of the Republic

11

charged in 1897 that no book then in use 'merits the unqualified endorsement of this organization.' "[2]

After World War I, a Hearst newspaper columnist warned Americans about "Anglicized" histories. That writer used a technique still used today: he counted the number of lines devoted to persons he liked and compared them to the number about persons he disliked. Then he expressed his outrage in print.

Various organizations attacked schoolbooks after World War I. The Daughters of the American Revolution denounced one American history because it did not "place enough emphasis on military history to make good soldiers out of children." The Veterans of Foreign Wars maintained by the end of the Twenties that the organization had "eliminated all of the objectionable features" in American histories and was turning its attention to modern European volumes. The Ku Klux Klan warned that the public school system was being attacked, through its textbooks, by "papists and anti-Christian Jews of the Bolshevik Socialist stripe." Anti-evolutionists attacked books that they maintained were filled with Darwinian ideas. Other groups expressed concern and exerted pressure on publishers against books that they considered to be too favorable toward unions or big business, too soft on socialism or communism, or too demeaning of the "founders of the Republic, or the men who preserved the union."[3]

Schoolbook pressures rose sharply after World War II. Individuals and organizations looked for books that treated communism favorably. In Indiana, a state senator tried to rid the entire state of *The Adventures of Robin Hood*, which she thought was a communist menace. Other groups became concerned with the new realism in novels that found their way into English classrooms. When Holden Caulfield checked into public schools across the nation, he brought trouble with him. Some teachers were fired for teaching about Holden's adolescent antics in *The Catcher in the Rye*. Other teachers considered the book to be a contemporary classic, began teaching it in the early Fifties, and have been teaching it without any negative comment ever since.

But nearly all of the schoolbook protests before the early Seventies were free of violence. Individuals and organizations became emotional about schoolbooks, and frequently heated words seared school board meetings and scorched the offices of publishers. But schoolbooks were not burned and people were not hurt.

In 1973, the school board in Drake, North Dakota, confiscated three books taught by a young English teacher. When the board ordered copies of Kurt Vonnegut's *Slaughterhouse Five* burned, there was a nationwide outrage about a book-burning in America. As a result, the Drake school board decided not to have copies of James Dickey's *Deliverance* and a volume of short stories thrown into the school's furnace.[4].

Less than a year after the book-burning in Drake, the United States experienced its first schoolbook war. The "battle of the books"[5] began when a first-term school board member and wife of a self-ordained minister launched a vigorous campaign against the English textbooks submitted for adoption in Kanawha County, West Virginia. To show their displeasure with the books, coal miners went on strike. Twenty-seven ministers denounced the books from their pulpits and in public meetings and rallies; 10 ministers supported the school board members who voted for the books. Snipers fired at school buses and, on one occasion, bullets hit a state police car that was escorting a bus filled with children. Gunmen wounded at least two persons and shot at others. Teachers repeatedly received threats on their lives. Textbook protesters firebombed an elementary school. Angry citizens dynamited at least three cars, vandalized school buses, and blasted windows in the board of education building with shotguns.[6] And the nation's most prominent schoolbook critics — Norma and Mel Gabler of Longview, Texas — flew to Charleston for what their biographer called "a whirlwind six-day speaking campaign"[7] against the 325 English language arts textbooks that had been tentatively approved by the Kanawha County school board.

A free-lance writer who reported on the nine-month dispute called it "in part a class war, a cultural war, a religious war. It is a struggle for power and authority that has sundered a peaceful community into rigid and fearful factions. And it is a complex and profoundly disturbing reflection of the deep fissures that crisscross American society."[8]

Since 1974, hundreds of less violent skirmishes over textbooks, films, tradebooks, courses, and teaching methods used in the nation's schools have "sundered peaceful communities." Disputes over classroom and library materials have erupted in every state, in rural as well as metropolitan school districts, in inner-city and suburban neighborhoods. The battles have left long-lasting scars and, in many instances, wounds that will never heal.

### 3. Is there evidence to support the claim that the number of incidents of schoolbook protest is rising annually?

Since 1966 Lee Burress, professor of English at the University of Wisconsin-Stevens Point, has been conducting surveys of attempts to censor school library and classroom materials. His fourth national survey, conducted in 1982, indicated that 34% of those surveyed reported challenges to books. The previous high was 30% in 1977. The 1973 figure was 28%; and the first figure he reported, in 1966, was 20%.[1]

In a conversation with me in 1982, Professor Burress predicted, based on the results of his surveys, that three out of five teachers of English in Wisconsin alone would experience attempts to censor classroom materials within five years. He noted that his 1982 survey yielded a fact he had not uncovered before: 17% of the respondents noted the involvement of locally organized pressure groups in attempts to remove materials from libraries and classrooms. He reported that in previous surveys the figure had been less than 1%.[2]

Another source of data on schoolbook protest activity is the Office of Intellectual Freedom (OIF) of the American Library Association. During the early Seventies, approximately 100 censorship incidents were reported yearly to the OIF. By 1976 the figure had risen to slightly less than 200 and climbed to nearly 300 in 1977.[3] Shortly after the 1980 presidential election, Judith F. Krug, director of the OIF, reported a fivefold increase in censorship incidents reported to her office. She later revised her estimate to a threefold increase, which would mean roughly 900 reported incidents a year.[4]

The results of a survey conducted by three professional organizations in 1980 indicate that the number of challenges to school library and classroom materials had increased from 1 September 1978 until the date of the survey. The report on the survey included these statements:

> *More than one in five (22.4%) of the 1,891 respondents, overall* — or nearly one administrator in five (19.2%) and nearly one librarian in three (29.5%) — *reported that there had been some challenges to classroom or library materials* in their school(s) during the period since September 1, 1978.

> *Of 494 respondents reporting challenges,* half (50.6%) found the rate of such incidents unchanged between the 1976-1978 and 1978-1980 periods, but *one in four (26.5%) indicated that the rate of challenges was higher in the more recent period* (as compared with 9.1% who responded "lower," and 13.8% who were "not certain").[5]

In Oregon, 60% of the respondents to a survey conducted by the Oregon Educational Media Association reported challenges to classroom and school library materials during the period from 1977 to 1982.[6] Surveying the same period, 1977-1982, the Association for Indiana Media Educators reported that 47% of the respondents had experienced one or more challenges to classroom and school library materials. Slightly more than 30% of the Indiana librarians reported three or more challenges during the five-year period.[7] The results of a survey conducted by the Ohio Council International Reading Association indicated that 46% of the responding elementary school teachers, librarians, and administrators reported attempts to remove classroom and school library materials during the previous year.[8]

In its two national surveys, People for the American Way discovered "attempts to remove, alter, or restrict students' access to a wide variety of educational materials in 48 of the 50 states." In the preface to its 1983-84 report, People for the American Way noted that:

> during the past school year censorship activity was widespread, pervasive, and better organized than ever before. It was initiated by a variety of sources: parents, teachers, school officials, school board members, librarians, civic groups, publishers, local clergy and church groups. In at least 20 percent of the incidents reported in 1983-84, local protest groups received assistance from nationally organized Far Right censorship groups such as Phyllis Schlafly's Eagle Forum, the national Pro-Family Forum, Mel and

Norma Gabler's Educational Research Analysts, Jerry Falwell's Moral Majority, and Tim and Beverly LaHaye's Concerned Women for America.[9]

But reported incidents represent only a small portion of the number of actual schoolbook protests each year. For every incident that is reported, some scholars estimate that 25 go unreported. As more and more data are gathered, other scholars estimate that the unreported-reported ratio is closer to 50 to one.

## 4. Why do the schoolbook protesters maintain that they are not censors?

During two different appearances on *Donahue*, Norma and Mel Gabler (see question 19) strongly denied that they are censors.[1] In her radio, television, and public appearances, Mrs. Gabler frequently points out that "only people in authority" can censor books. She maintains that she and her husband "only have a voice" in the textbook selection process in Texas. She notes that her "right to dissent" has been called censorship; and that, she believes, is wrong. Mel Gabler points out that the authors, editors, and publishers are the "real censors" who "have already censored out" of textbooks "all that is good, beautiful, true, helpful, and friendly."[2]

The Gablers are not alone in expressing their disdain for the term censorship when it is applied to what they do. All of the schoolbook protesters I have met — from the political and religious right or left — proclaim that they are not censors. They rely on these dictionary definitions to support their assertion: an official who examines publications for objectionable matter; an official who reads communications and deletes forbidden material.

Additional definitions are needed to describe today's activities. People who call for the removal of books, people who want the classrooms cleansed of everything they do not like, people who travel the country urging others to rid the schools of "objectionable" content — such people may be appropriately called censors whether they like the term or not.

Six years ago I included the names of two organizations and a very brief description of some of their activities in a chapter that I wrote for a book on censorship. The leaders of the organizations were enraged. One wrote to the publisher of the book, demanding that the publisher "shut Ed Jenkinson up." The organization then insisted it had never been involved in any activity that could be called censorship. The second organization sent a telegram to the publisher, urging it to cease distributing the book immediately and proclaiming that the protesting organization had never been involved in any censorious activity.

Censors do not seem to recognize their own work.

The words *censor* and *censorship* have strong negative connotations, and schoolbook protesters who demand the removal of books by applying pressure on persons in authority dislike those words. (See question 5.)

## 5. What is censorship when that term is applied to school materials?

Censorship is any act intended to keep students from reading, seeing, or hearing any materials that some person deems objectionable. It is also the attempt to rid the schools of courses, teaching methods, and ideas. It takes many forms, including these:

1. The removal of books — without submitting them to a full review process — from classrooms or libraries because someone called the books objectionable (see questions 33, 37, and 39). It is an all too common practice in America for someone to object to a book without having read it — or without even having seen it. Unfortunately, it is not unusual for a person in authority — superintendent, school board member, principal, teacher, or librarian — to remove a challenged book without having read it or having submitted it to a duly authorized review committee.

2. The blacking out of words with a felt-tip pen or other instrument. An English teacher used a felt-tip pen to cover the word *crap* in all

of the copies of an English literature anthology. She would have been disappointed with the results of her work had she heard the students guess which word was blacked out. Not a one thought the offensive word was *crap*. Razor blades and scissors also are used to remove words or passages.

3. The gluing together of pages that someone considered to be offensive. An administrator pasted together the few pages dealing with sex in a health textbook. The community indicated that it did not approve of his action.

4. One administrator commissioned an artist to put shorts on the little boy who wanders around in the nude in Maurice Sendak's very popular *In the Night Kitchen*.

5. A school board member admitted that she checked out of the school library the books that she did not like, and then failed to return them. Rather, she sent the librarian a check to cover the cost of the books. She was severely reprimanded for her actions.

6. A principal told me that he had never experienced censorship in his 30 years as an administrator. Then he paused and confided: "Oh, once a minister complained about a book of mythology. I think it was the one by Edith Hamilton. Anyway, the minister got so angry about the book that I just took it out of the library when the school was closed and threw it in the furnace." An elementary school librarian became concerned when she noted a very high number of missing books. Through quiet investigation and observation she discovered that the principal removed any book that a citizen objected to and threw it in the fire. He apparently never questioned any challenger nor defended a book; he simply destroyed it.

7. In Texas, persons who challenge the textbooks submitted for adoption write Bills of Particulars in which they cite objections, line by line, paragraph by paragraph. If the Texas Commissioner of Education, after consulting with the board, agrees with any of the objections, he informs the publisher to make changes before the books are adopted (see questions 19, 20, and 21).

8. Protest groups exert pressure on publishers to keep certain materials out of books (evolution, for example). Publishers, in turn, may tell authors to avoid writing about certain "objectionable" ideas. This is prior restraint.

9. Teachers and librarians practice self-censorship when they refuse to teach a book or order one because they discover that it has been challenged elsewhere.

10. Legislators at the state or national level practice censorship when they prepare and pass legislation designed to keep certain courses and books out of the public schools (see question 30).

## 6. What are some of the results of attempts to remove teaching materials from public schools?

Censorship has a chilling effect on the academic climate in a school during and after an incident. Commenting on the Warsaw, Indiana, incident, a counselor noted that teachers were afraid to discuss controversial issues for several years after the school board turned a classroom set of textbooks over to senior citizens for a public burning and after the board dismissed two teachers. He said that the quality of education suffered as a result.[1] Similar comments have been made about the results of censorship incidents in other communities. (For a partial listing of censorship incidents, see question 15.)

One result of censorship that does not please schoolbook protesters is that censored books or other materials frequently become best sellers among the very persons who were not supposed to read them. In Warsaw, Indiana, for example, students told me that they drove as far as 60 miles to other school districts to get a copy of Sidney Simon's *Values Clarification*, the textbook that had been burned. The author of *365 Days*, a book that had been banned in Baileyville, Maine, reported that 4,000 copies of the book were sold in Maine alone during the two months following the trial about the removal of the book.[2] (The court ordered the School Committee to return the book to the school library.) John Steinbeck's *Grapes of Wrath* became a best seller in Kanawha, Iowa, after it had been banned from two classes. "Bookstore managers and librarians in Kanawha and surrounding Iowa communities reported that readers grabbed every copy in sight. The Kanawha Public Library, which owns only one copy of the 1939 novel, borrowed a dozen copies to meet reader demand."[3]

## 7. What is the difference between censorship and selection? Between censorship and consciousness raising?

More than 30 years ago, Lester Asheim made this oft-quoted distinction between censorship and selection:

> Selection . . . begins with a presumption in favor of liberty of thought; censorship, with a presumption in favor of thought control. Selection's approach to the book is positive, seeking its value in the book as a book and in the book as a whole. Censorship's approach is negative, seeking for vulnerable characteristics wherever they can be found — anywhere within the book, or even outside it. Selection seeks to protect the right of the reader to read; censorship seeks to protect — not the right — but the reader himself from the fancied effects of his reading. The selector has faith in the intelligence of the reader; the censor has faith only in his own.
>
> In other words, selection is democratic while censorship is authoritarian, and in our democracy we have traditionally tended to put our trust in the selector rather than in the censor.[1]

Censors like to point out that there is little difference between selection and censorship. Or as one schoolbook protester noted on a *Donahue Show,* "One man's selection is another man's censorship."[2]

When he was state superintendent of schools in California, Max Rafferty wrote:

> All school people censor things all the time. We are speaking about educational censorship and, of course, in education we don't call it censorship, we call it screening. This is one of the things we professional schoolmen get paid for, and if we didn't do it, we would be out of a job.[3]

But there are these basic differences between censors and selectors:

| Censors | Selectors |
|---|---|
| Censors search for what they want to discard. | Selectors examine material, looking for that which best presents their educational objectives. |

| Censors judge a book on the basis of a few passages they dislike. | Selectors judge the book as a whole. |
|---|---|
| Censors rely on the reviews of other censors to get rid of books. | Selectors rely on reviews published in professional journals. |
| Censors know what is right for all people; therefore, they want books that represent their point of view. | Selectors look for books that represent a variety of points of view. |
| Censors look outside the book for reasons to reject it. For example, the author's religion or politics. | Selectors judge the book on its own merits. |

Julia T. Bradley, an attorney who wrote a detailed analysis of the distinctions between censorship and selection, concluded in her article for the *Connecticut Law Review*:

> Despite school board protestations to the contrary, censorship and selection are distinguishable. Censorship is an act whereby one group imposes its value judgment upon another and permanently limits access to certain resources. Selection, on the other hand, is a process; the only inherent constraint upon choosing among all published materials is that of budget. Where censorship occurs, decisions are absolute; a book is unsuitable. In the selection process, choices are relative; is this book more useful, for varied reasons, than another? Moreover, where censorship occurs, one group permanently terminates another's right to judge a book for itself. Where selection operates without restraints, a book which readers consider "bad" will die of neglect.[4]

Consciousness raising on the part of an individual or organization is an attempt to make textbooks and books for children more representative of women and minorities. Several professional organizations have requested that publishers establish guidelines so that women and minorities will be treated fairly and accurately.

One attempt at consciousness raising comes from the National Education Association in a brochure titled "How Fair Are Your Children's Textbooks." A portion of that brochure is printed below:

How fair are your children's textbooks? Not just history or social studies texts, but all the books they use. Students form ideas from everything they see — the stories in the primer, the examples in the spelling book, the illustrations in the math and natural science books, the selections and commentary in the literature books. Ask yourself the following questions about your children's textbooks:

Do they seem to assume a white, Christian audience?

Do they continue to romanticize American history, glorifying the "Manifest Destiny" of the westward movement and glossing over the fact that Indians and chicanos were "cleared" from their lands like trees in the way of "progress"?

Do minorities, when mentioned at all, appear as social problems to be solved rather than as valuable contributors to our pluralistic society?

Are Indians described in degrading "outgroup" terms *(roaming, ferocious, primitive)?* Are Indian defeats called *battles*, Indian victories *massacres*?

Do the stories in the readers feature suburban families of four, with briefcase-toting fathers and nonworking mothers? (Many children who cannot see anything familiar in such stories quite understandably decide that reading is not for them.)

Are problems in the math books illustrated with pictures showing boys earning money and building things, while girls spend money, cook, and sew?

Do the history books hail pre-1880 immigrants to America as *pioneers* and *settlers* and describe later arrivals (particularly non-Europeans) as *swarms* and *teeming hordes*?

Do the authors try to give a "balanced" treatment of the "pros and cons" of slavery? (This is about as acceptable as a "balanced" treatment of Nazism would be.)

Do the illustrations in the readers and social studies texts fail to show minority group members or women in positions of authority or power?

Do world history books first mention Africa in connection with the slave trade, neglecting its great early civilizations?

Do the evolution charts in the biology texts end with a white male, as if he were somehow more truly evolution's end product than a woman, or a black man, or an Indian, or a chicano, or an Oriental?

Do the history and social studies texts still advance the melting pot theory, whereby all minority groups are expected to "melt" into the ways of the majority? (The truth of our national character is *multiculturalism*; uniculturalism is a myth.)

Do "revised" textbooks offer only tokenism (tinting of Caucasian features in illustrations or perfunctory inclusion of the same few black heroes, as if no others existed)?

If your answer to questions like these is yes, the myths are being advanced, and reality is being avoided.[5]

Where does consciousness raising end and censorship begin? That question troubles scholars who study attempts to censor school materials. When persons involved in consciousness raising call — either overtly or covertly — for the removal of books, they have crossed the line and have begun acting like censors. When such persons demand that certain works not be published, they have practiced prior restraint, which is a form of censorship.

## 8. Can censorship of school materials ever be good?

Some persons argue that since challenges to books sometimes cause teachers to re-examine what they are doing, the results are good. If a protest results in a publisher's revising a book to accommodate the protester's complaint, then some would say that censorship is good. Others argue that censorship has a negative, "chilling" effect on the academic climate and is therefore bad.

Censorship incidents tend to become intensely emotional conflicts. Both sides frequently get hurt in a variety of ways. Communities become divided. "Friends" sometimes stop speaking to members of either party in the conflict. Wounds are slow to heal and leave long-lasting scars.

I have talked with at least 60 teachers, librarians, administrators, school board members, parents, and students who have been involved in some form of schoolbook protest — either as a protester or as a defender of a book, a teaching method, a film, or a course. All indicated that they wanted to forget the experience but found it very hard to do so. At least half of the teachers with whom I talked have left the teaching profession. Unfortunately for the profession, all were good — some even excellent — teachers. (See questions 2 and 32.)

Attempts to prevent students from reading certain materials altogether may have an effect opposite to the one the censors wanted. Students who might not otherwise read a specific book will frequently do so if it is banned. (See question 6.)

## 9. Why do opponents of the schoolbook protest movement invoke the First Amendment?

The Supreme Court affirmed the constitutional rights of students and teachers, and specifically the protection of the First Amendment, in the landmark case of *Tinker* v. *Des Moines Independent Community School District*,[1] which involved three students who were suspended for wearing black armbands to protest the U.S. government's policy in Vietnam. The Supreme Court made this frequently quoted statement: "It can hardly be argued that either students or teachers shed their constitutional rights to freedom of speech or expression at the schoolhouse gate."[2]

The limiting of access to knowledge in a school library becomes a First Amendment issue (see question 12). The student's rights to know and the teacher's right to academic freedom are also First Amendment issues (see questions 10 and 11).

## 10. What are the students' rights to learn?

All children in the United States have a right — indeed, an obligation — to attend school for about 10 years. "Courts have recognized that the right to an education is fundamental and that the removal of a student from school is a severe punishment, which school officials have the right to administer only in cases of serious wrongdoing and only with strict safeguards against arbitrariness and unfairness."[1] The courts also have recognized, in some instances, that the "right to an education means the right to a good education."[2]

In 1924 the Supreme Court ruled that parents have the right to direct the education of their children,[3] and it essentially reaffirmed that right in a 1972 decision.[4] But the Supreme Court also has recognized that students have constitutional rights. *Tinker v. Des Moines Independent Community School District* stands as the beacon, signalling that students have protected constitutional rights and — specifically in this case — protected First Amendment rights. Four passages from the *Tinker* decision have special significance in the consideration of student rights:

> It can hardly be argued that either students or teachers shed their constitutional rights to freedom of speech or expression at the schoolhouse gate.
>
> The District Court concluded that the action of the school authorities was reasonable because it was based on their fear of a disturbance from the wearing of the armbands. But, in our system, undifferentiated fear or apprehension of disturbance is not enough to overcome the right to freedom of expression. Any departure from absolute regimentation may cause trouble. Any variation from the majority's opinion may inspire fear. Any word spoken, in class, in the lunchroom, or on the campus, that deviates from the views of another person may start an argument or cause a disturbance. But our Constitution says that we must take this risk, and our history says that it is this sort of hazardous freedom — this kind of openness — that is the basis of our national strength and of the independence and vigor of Americans who grow up and live in this relatively permissive, often disputatious, society.
>
> In order for the state in the person of school officials to justify prohibition of a particular expression of opinion, it must be able

to show that its action was caused by something more than a mere desire to avoid the discomfort and unpleasantness that always accompany an unpopular viewpoint. Certainly where there is no finding and no showing that engaging in the forbidden conduct would "materially and substantially interfere with the requirements of appropriate discipline in the operation of the school," the prohibition cannot be sustained.

In our system, state-operated schools may not be enclaves of totalitarianism. School officials do not possess absolute authority over their students. Students in school as well as out of school are "persons" under our Constitution. They are possessed of fundamental rights which the State must respect, just as they themselves must respect their obligations to the State. In our system, students may not be regarded as closed-circuit recipients of only that which the State chooses to communicate. They may not be confined to the expression of those sentiments that are officially approved. In the absence of a specific showing of constitutionally valid reasons to regulate their speech, students are entitled to freedom of expression of their views.[5]

Protected First Amendment rights, as designated in *Tinker* and other cases, provide students with the rights "to know" and to read. As attorney Julia T. Bradley notes: "A student's right to read, and thus to have available in a school library a full range of materials which reflect differing literary styles, and differing social, political, and religious views, is a variant of a constitutional doctrine described as the 'right to receive information'."[6] As a result of her reading of case law, Bradley states: "Students can challenge a school board's removal of a book from the school library not because they have the right to read that particular work from that particular outlet, but because the book represents their right not to have access to books made more difficult or choices of reading material restricted arbitrarily."[7]

The courts' recognition of the student's protected constitutional rights, independent of the rights of parents to direct the education of their children, has resulted in situations in which two sets of rights have come into conflict. The rights of students have also precipitated conflicts with school boards and school administrators who have not been fully cognizant of the courts' current attention to those rights. (See questions 11, 12, and 13.)

In one Supreme Court case involving the First Amendment, Justice Louis Brandeis included the following statement of James Madison, which is relevant to the First Amendment rights of students:

> Knowledge will forever govern ignorance; and a people who mean to be their own Governors, must arm themselves with the power which knowledge gives. A popular government without popular information or the means of acquiring it, is but a prologue to farce or tragedy, or, perhaps both.[8]

## 11. What is academic freedom? Does it apply to elementary and secondary school teachers? And what have the courts said about academic freedom for public school teachers?

Until the 1960s the courts had not been involved in the issue of academic freedom for public school teachers. Academic freedom was primarily considered as a right of college professors. But recently the courts have ruled in a few cases whether teachers should have the right to control course content, course materials, and teaching methods. And public school teachers have gone to court to determine the extent of their rights to teach and to express themselves.

Critics of academic freedom for public school teachers like to quote these three sentences from the judge's decision in *Mailloux* v. *Kiley*: "The faculty of a secondary school does not have the independent traditions, the broad discretions as to teaching methods, not usually the intellectual qualifications, of university professors. Among secondary school teachers there are often many persons with little experience. Some teachers and most students have limited intellectual and emotional maturity."[1] The judge also said: "Most parents, students, school boards, and members of the community usually expect the secondary school to concentrate on transmitting basic information, teaching 'the best that is known and thought in the world,' training by established techniques, and, to some extent at least, indoctrinating in the *mores* of the surrounding society." The judge noted that secondary schools are not "open forums in which mature adults, already habituated to social restraints, exchange ideas on a level of parity." The judge expressed his opinion that "it cannot be accepted as a premise that the student is voluntarily in the classroom and willing to be exposed to a teaching method which, though reasonable, is not approved by the school authorities or by the weight of professional opinion."[2]

Mailloux, the teacher plaintiff, was not dismissed, however. The judge held that the "attempted dismissal of Mailloux violated the constitutional procedural right recognized by *Keefe* and *Parducci* — the right of a teacher not to be dismissed for using a 'reasonable' teaching method unless he or she has been put on notice not to use that method."[3]

In a frequently quoted article in a law journal, Stephen R. Goldstein challenged academic freedom for secondary school teachers. He wrote that "cases involving restrictions on teachers' rights of curricular control are often erroneously viewed as censorship cases when the real issue is who should make curricular choices given the fact that someone has to make choices. With regard to this issue, the arguments that the Constitution allocates curricular decision making authority to the teacher are not persuasive."[4]

Goldstein rejected both professionalism and the First Amendment as arguments in behalf of academic freedom for public school teachers. In refuting the First Amendment argument, he wrote: "The freedom of expression justification for teacher control is premised on an analytical model of education which views school as a market place of ideas. There is no historical or precedential basis, however, for concluding that the market place of ideas model is constitutionally compelled over the traditional value inculcation model. Thus, in the final analysis, teachers' constitutional rights, in and out of the classroom, do not extend beyond the First Amendment rights of all citizens."[5]

In a significant case involving academic freedom of secondary school teachers, Judge Richard P. Matsch refuted Goldstein's argument with these words: "To restrict the opportunity for involvement in an open forum for the free exchange of ideas would not only foster an unacceptable elitism, it would also fail to complete the development of those not going on to college, contrary to our constitutional commitment to equal opportunity. Effective citizenship in a participatory democracy must not be dependent upon advancement toward college degrees.

Consequently, it would be inappropriate to conclude that academic freedom is required only in the colleges and universities."[6]

Judge Matsch refuted Goldstein's argument that teachers are "essentially, extensions of their employers." If teachers must follow only the wishes of the majority as reflected by the school board and school authorities, the result would be tyranny. "The tyranny of the majority is as contrary to the fundamental principles of the Constitution as the authoritarianism of an autocracy."[7]

The U.S. Supreme Court has yet to hear a case involving academic freedom in the public schools, but the lower courts have begun to recognize the need for academic freedom in the schools. Two cases are particularly significant. In *Keefe* v. *Geanakos*, the First Circuit Court held that a teacher had been improperly dismissed for assigning an *Atlantic Monthly* article that contained a taboo word. The court concluded that the principles of academic freedom embodied in the Constitution barred the teacher's dismissal.[8] In its decision, the court included this quotation from the Supreme Court case of *Wiemann* v. *Updegraff*: "Such unwarranted inhibition upon the free spirit of teachers affects not only those who . . . are immediately before the Court. It has an unmistakable tendency to chill that free play of the spirit which all teachers ought especially to cultivate and practice."[9]

In *Parducci* v. *Rutland*, a high school teacher of English was dismissed for being insubordinate when she refused to comply with superiors' orders that she never again teach Kurt Vonnegut's short story, "Welcome to the Monkey House."[10] Two of the administrators in the school district called the story "literary garbage," and they claimed that its philosophy favored killing off old people and advocated free sex. They also told the teacher that three students asked to be excused from the assignment and that several parents complained about the story. When the teacher did not follow the administrators' orders, the school board dismissed her on the grounds that the story had a "disruptive effect" on the school, and that she had refused "counseling and advice of the school principal," and was therefore guilty of "insubordination."[11]

The court upheld the teacher's right to teach the story and denied the school board the right to dismiss her. The court found that the story was appropriate for high school juniors and that it was not obscene. The court also noted that Vonnegut was not advocating killing the elderly but that he was satirizing the depersonalization of man in society.[12] In *Parducci*, the court partially answered this question: Should school officials have the power to decide what should be taught and what should be banned? The court declared that the Vonnegut story, as judged by other works that the students read in and out of school, was not obscene. The court also found that the assignment of the short story was not disruptive to the school; in fact, the court noted that it was met with apathy by most of the students, except the three who asked to be excused from the assignment.[13]

The courts have begun to recognize that the First Amendment provides a measure of academic freedom for public school teachers. The courts also have attempted to balance the rights of teachers, parents, students, and the state.[14] Noting that the courts have treated academic freedom for public school teachers more as a protected "interest" than a "right," Martha M. McCarthy and Nelda H. Cambron caution that the courts have preferred to view each case individually. "Therefore, teachers must rely on the various judicial decisions for general guidance only." And teachers should be "aware of the relationship between the particular materials or teaching methods employed and the course being taught. If methods or materials are completely unrelated to course objectives, their use would not be viewed as legally protected."[15]

The courts have not always decided in favor of teachers and their claim to academic freedom — particularly when the teachers have departed from their assigned subject matter or have used unacceptable teaching methods. For example, the courts have decided that a teacher could not discuss sex in an all-male speech class,[16] that a teacher could not discuss politics in an economics class,[17] that a teacher could not discuss his disapproval of ROTC in an algebra class,[18] and that teachers have no constitutional rights to use unorthodox teaching methods.[19]

## 12. How have the courts responded to the censorship of school materials?

Human beings preside in the courts, and human beings do not agree on all matters. Thus it is not surprising that the courts have not been uniform in their decisions involving the removal of books and other teaching materials from public school classrooms and libraries. The courts do tend to agree that they prefer not to become involved in debates over educational objectives and practices, leaving such matters to school boards, unless they believe that specific constitutional rights have been violated. But when they do become involved, their decisions are not always predictable, as the following brief consideration of selected cases indicates.

Piri Thomas portrayed Harlem as a very unpleasant place to live in *Down These Mean Streets.* He used language and described incidents that provoked a group of parents in New York's School District 25 to request that the book be removed from the shelves of several school libraries. In response to the request, the district board conducted an open hearing in which all but two of 73 speakers favored retention of the book, either on literary or educational grounds. But the board voted 5 to 3 to remove the book from the district's junior high school libraries. Six weeks after the superintendent carried out the board's order, the board modified its decision in a public meeting. The board said that libraries that had purchased the book could keep it, but it limited the loan of the book to parents of students attending the schools — not to the students themselves.[1]

The district court dismissed, without a hearing, a complaint about restricting the circulation of the book filed by a group of parents, teachers, students, and a school librarian. The Second Circuit Court of Appeals unanimously affirmed the lower court's decision, noting no violation of constitutional rights and stating that someone had to take the responsibility for determining what will be in a library collection. It also observed that shouts of book burning could hardly elevate an "intramural strife to first amendment constitutional proportions." Otherwise, "there would be a constant intrusion of the judiciary into the internal affairs of the school."[2]

When the plaintiffs appealed the Second Circuit Court's decision, the Supreme Court refused to review the case. In his dissenting opinion, Justice William O. Douglas made a telling point when he wrote: "What else can the School Board now decide it does not like? How else will its sensibilities be offended? Are we sending children to school to be educated by the norms of the School Board or are we educating our youth to shed the prejudices of the past, to explore all forms of thought, and to find solutions to our world's problems?"[3]

The above case, *President's Council, District 25* v. *Community School Bd. No 25*, is cited frequently by those who attempt to have books removed from libraries and classrooms. But according to students of the First Amendment, the case did not answer the crucial questions in such matters since the courts chose to treat the incident as a matter of shelving and unshelving books. In his analysis of the decision, Robert M. O'Neil, president of the University of Virginia, observed that the "insensitivity of the Second Circuit's disposition . . . is understandable . . . because the case was one of first impression. The simple fact is that no constitutional decisions have defined the relative rights and responsibilities of public libraries and their patrons."[4] In a law journal article, O'Neil concluded: "If the citizenry is to be fully informed and if the primary functions of government are to be exercised by a responsible and knowledgeable electorate, then the library should be as unfettered as the press, the broadcast media, and the universities."[5]

Writing in the *Connecticut Law Review*, Julia T. Bradley made these observations about *President's Council*:

> The court, in focusing on the issue of "who should decide," failed to discuss the substantive nature of the board's decision. As a result, *President's Council* is insensitive to the realities of the situation. *Down These Mean Streets* had been chosen to expose its readers to an environment unlike their own. The board removed the book solely because its colloquial language and descriptions of unpleasant scenes offended some people in the community.
>
> The *President's Council* opinion sidesteps the constitutional issue: What are proper criteria under the first amendment for choosing or removing books from a school library? While not capable of precise definition, general guidelines can be established. For example, the final decisionmaker should use standards based on the usefulness of a book in relation to the educational needs of

students. Arbitrary criteria, such as personal dislike of a book's language or ideas or unsubstantiated fear of some harmful effect, should be disregarded. Because it ignored these questions, *President's Council* is an inadequate guide for courts facing other incidents of censorship in school libraries."[6]

The second and only other case involving a censorship incident that has gone to the Supreme Court is *Pico* v. *Board of Education, Island Trees Union Free School District*. This case involved an incident on Long Island, not far from the site of the *President's Council* case. However, in *Pico* 11 books, including *Down These Mean Streets*, were involved. After three members of the school board of Island Trees attended a meeting of Parents of New York - United (PONY-U), the school board voted to remove these 11 books from school libraries: *Go Ask Alice* by Anonymous, *A Reader for Writers* edited by Jerome W. Archer, *A Hero Ain't Nothin' but a Sandwich* by Alice Childress, *Soul on Ice* by Eldridge Cleaver, *Best Short Stories by Negro Writers* by Langston Hughes, *Laughing Boy* by Oliver La Farge, *The Fixer* by Bernard Malamud, *The Naked Ape* by Desmond Morris, *Down These Mean Streets* by Piri Thomas, *Slaughterhouse Five* by Kurt Vonnegut, and *Black Boy* by Richard Wright.

At the PONY-U meeting, the board members said they "learned of books found in schools throughout the country which were anti-American, anti-Christian, anti-Semitic and just plain filthy."[7] Two board members entered a school library at night and looked through the card catalog to determine that nine of the books were available. The board gave lists of the objectionable books to the school librarians and ordered them to remove the titles from the shelves. On learning that Bernard Malamud's *The Fixer* was used in an English class, the principal removed all copies from the classroom and storage closet. *Laughing Boy* and *A Reader for Writers*, the two books available in the junior high school library, were removed from the shelves.[8]

The school board did not follow its own policies for reviewing and removing books from classrooms or libraries. The board's action stirred sufficient controversy in the community to cause it to appoint a committee of four parents and four teachers to review the books. As a result of the recommendation of the review committee, the board returned two titles, *Laughing Boy* and *Black Boy*, to the school library but removed all others despite the review committee's vote to retain *Go Ask Alice, The Fixer,* and *Best Short Stories by Negro Writers.* The board also restricted access to *Black Boy* to those students who had written permission from their parents to borrow the book.[9]

Five students in the Island Trees district filed suit against the school board in the U.S. District Court for the Eastern District of New York. The suit claimed that the board, by removing nine books from school libraries, violated both New York and U.S. constitutional guarantees of freedom of expression. In an *amicus* brief filed by the American Jewish Committee and other organizations, the authors of the brief noted that they were astounded that *The Fixer* "was banned because it contained anti-Semitic references. That assertion can lead to only one of two conclusions: that its author is either illiterate or dishonest. *The Fixer* clearly condemns anti-Semitism, as it does the authoritarian society which is the seed bed of anti-Semitism."[10]

The district court judge relied heavily on *President's Council* to rule in favor of the defendant school board. Judge George C. Pratt observed:

> Here, the Island Trees school board removed certain books because it viewed them as vulgar and in bad taste, a removal that clearly was content-based. Whether they were correct in their evaluation of the books is not the issue. Nor is the issue whether, assuming the books to be vulgar and in bad taste, it is a wise or even desirable educational decision to sanitize the library by removing them, thereby sheltering the students from their influence. Such issues should be decided and remedied either by the school district's voters, or by the State Commissioner of Education on an appropriate administrative level.
>
> Here, the issue is whether the First Amendment requires a federal court to forbid a school board from removing library books which its members find to be inconsistent with the basic values of the community that elected them. *President's Council* resolved that issue by holding that a book that was improperly selected "for whatever reason" could be removed "by the same authority which was empowered to make the selection in the first place."[11]

In a 2 to 1 decision, the Second Circuit Court reversed the decision of the district court and remanded the case for trial. But the school board appealed the decision and the Supreme Court accepted the case — the first of its kind to have a hearing before the high Court. Anticipating a decision that would affect school libraries and classrooms for years, teachers, librarians, administrators, and students of the First Amendment who had followed the case awaited the Supreme Court decision and hoped for a decision that would give guidance to the education profession. Their hopes were denied.

Nearly seven years after the initial action that precipitated *Pico*, the Supreme Court handed down its split decision on 25 June 1982. Writing about the split decision of the court, R. Bruce Rich, counsel to the Association of American Publishers Freedom to Read Committee, observed:

> The case posed for the Court the issue of whether and, if so, in what circumstances . . . book removals in the school setting can deprive students of their First Amendment rights. Not surprisingly, the Court divided sharply on the issue, with the decision reflected in seven separate opinions, none of which commanded a majority of the Justices. Nevertheless, a majority of the Court voted to return the case for further trial proceedings to determine the underlying motivations of the local school board in removing the books, thereby preserving the First Amendment claims of the students and rejecting the notion that there are no potential constitutional constraints on school board actions in this area. Viewed in this light, the decision, for all its uncertainties, must be regarded as a significant victory for the proponents of a vigorous First Amendment and of the freedom to read.[12]

In the *Newsletter on Intellectual Freedom* of the American Library Association, R. Bruce Rich made these comments on the significance of the decision:

> If nothing else, the *Island Trees* decision sends an important message to school officials who may be intent on cleansing school library shelves of works which they view as personally offensive. That message is that such actions will be subject to searching scrutiny — in the federal courts if necessary — to assure that they are properly motivated. More generally, by preserving the students' constitutional claims, the Court placed school library book removals within the class of official conduct in the school setting which is subject to First Amendment limitations.
>
> At the same time, it is important to recognize that the decision contains a number of self-stated limitations, as well as ambigui-

ties. It is thus unclear what, if any, constitutional limitations attend a school system's textbook acquisition decisions, or its library acquisition policies. In this connection, one must wonder how absolutely Justice Brennan intended his statement that "[Local school boards] might well defend their claim of absolute discretion in matters of curriculum by reliance upon their duty to inculcate community values."

Equally unclear is the meaning of such concepts as "pervasive vulgarity" and "educational suitability" as rationales for book removals. Could such terms not be used by a school board intent on developing a "proper" record to justify a vast range of questionable book removals?

Similarly left unclear by the decision is the extent to which procedures must be adopted and adhered to in connection with book removals. Are such procedures a constitutional requirement or is a failure to utilize procedures merely a factor which the courts will examine in evaluating the motivation underlying particular removals?

These and other unresolved issues may or may not be clarified by subsequent court decisions . . . . In the meanwhile, librarians, publishers and others committed to the First Amendment principles at stake in this area can be pleased that the Supreme Court — even if in less than compelling fashion — has recognized and preserved those principles.[13]

The Supreme Court may not choose to hear another book removal case in this decade, or in this century, but such cases will undoubtedly be tried in the lower courts. Therefore, an examination of several significant lower court decisions may prove useful.

In *Minarcini* v. *Strongsville City School District* five high school students challenged the school board's right to determine what books could be selected as textbooks, what books could be selected for the school library, which books could be removed from the school library, and which books could be banned from the high school classroom.

The Sixth Circuit Court upheld the school board's right to decide which books could be approved as textbooks, but it denied the school board the right to remove previously purchased library books. The Sixth Circuit Court observed:

the court must conclude that the board removed the books Kurt Vonnegut's *Cat's Cradle* and Joseph Heller's *Catch-22* because it found them objectionable in content and because it felt it had the power, unfettered by the First Amendment, to censor the school library for subject matter that the board members found distasteful. . . . A public library is a valuable adjunct to classroom discussion. If a teacher considered Joseph Heller's *Catch-22* to be an important American novel, no one would dispute that the First Amendment's protection of academic freedom would protect both his right to say so in class and his student's right to hear him and to find and read the book. Obviously, the student's success in this last endeavor would be greatly hindered by the fact that the book had been removed from the school library. The removal of books from a school library is a much more serious burden upon freedom of classroom discussion than the action found unconstitutional in *Tinker* v. *Des Moines* . . . . This burden is not minimized by the availability of the disputed book in sources outside the school. [14]

In *Right to Read Defense Committee of Chelsea* v. *School Committee of the City of Chelsea* the president of the Chelsea (Massachusetts) School Committee objected to *Male and Female Under 18*, a book that a parent brought to the president's attention. As editor of the local newspaper, the president immediately denounced the book in his newspaper even though he had not read any part of the anthology of prose and poetry written by high school students.

Throughout his decision, Judge Joseph Tauro quoted from editorials and news stories in the Chelsea newspaper to underscore the arbitrariness of the president of the school committee in having the book removed from the school library. The judge ordered the book returned to the library, noting that in a school library "a student can literally explore the unknown, and discover areas of interest and thought not covered by the prescribed curriculum. The student who discovers the magic of the library is on the way to a life-long experience of self-education and enrichment. That student learns that a library is a place to test or expand upon ideas presented to him, in or out of the classroom. The most effective antidote to the poison of mindless orthodoxy is ready access to a broad sweep of ideas and philosophies. There is no danger in such exposure. The danger is in mind control."[15]

In *Salvail* v. *Nashua Board of Education* one member of the Nashua (New Hampshire) School Board asked that *Ms. Magazine* be removed from the high school library because it contained advertisements for contraceptives, vibrators, materials dealing with lesbianism and witchcraft, and gay material. He also objected to advertisements for what he described as a pro-communist newspaper (*The Guardian*) and advertisements suggesting trips to Cuba. In addition he felt that the magazine encouraged students and teachers to send away for records made by known communist folk singers. Another school board member who was a former principal said that the "proper test for material to be available for reading by high school students was whether it could be read aloud to his daughter in a classroom."

The school board voted to remove back issues of *Ms. Magazine* from the high school library and to cancel the subscription. The school board ignored the procedures for handling complaints about school materials that had been distributed to all New Hampshire school districts by the State Department of Education. Members of the board felt they were not bound by New Hampshire's interim guidelines and that "in some cases they should act instantaneously."

The court ordered the school board to return the magazine to the library shelves and to renew the subscription. The court observed: "despite protestations contained in the testimony of these parties, it is the 'political' content of *Ms. Magazine* more than its sexual overtones that led to its arbitrary displacement. Such a basis for removal of the publication is constitutionally impermissible."[16]

*Bicknell* v. *Vergennes Union High School Board of Directors* grew out of an ongoing controversy concerning some of the books in the Vergennes (Vermont) Union High School library. The board of directors established a written policy governing the selection and removal of books that specified the "rights and responsibilities" of the board, the professional staff, the parents, and the students. The "rights" of the board are: "To adopt policy and procedure, consistent with statute and regulation — that they feel is in the best interests of students, parents, teachers and community." For professional staff: "To freely select, in accordance with Board policy, organize and administer the media collection to best serve teachers and students." For students: "To freely exercise the right to read and to free access to library materials." The policy also includes procedures and criteria for the selection of materials and a procedure allowing parents to submit requests for review of books. The procedure calls for the librarian to meet with the parents to resolve the issue; unresolved matters go to the board.

Several months after the adoption of the policy, parents complained about two books, Patrick Mann's *Dog Day Afternoon* and Richard Price's *The Wanderers*. The parents objected to "the vulgarity and indecency of language" in the books. The board voted to remove *The Wanderers* and to place *Dog Day Afternoon* on a restricted shelf. The board also voted to prohibit the school librarian from purchasing any additional major works of fiction, and subsequently voted that any book purchases other than those in the categories "Dorothy Canfield Fisher, science fiction and high interest-low vocabulary must be reviewed by the school administration in consultation with the Board." A group of students, their parents, and other parents filed a complaint asking the district court in Vermont to enjoin the removal of the books and the alteration of the policy.

The Second Circuit Court upheld the decision of the lower court that the removal of the books did not constitute a suppression of ideas and thus was not a violation of First Amendment rights of students. Nor did the board's changing of the procedures constitute a violation of due process.[17]

It is interesting to note that the Second Circuit Court delivered this opinion on the same day that it decided against the school board in *Pico*.

In *Zykan v. Warsaw Community School Corporation* Brooke and Blair Zykan sued the Warsaw (Indiana) School Board for violating their First Amendment rights as students by these actions: 1) removing an elective course titled "Values for Everyone" from the curriculum and turning the class set of *Values Clarification* over to a group of senior citizens for a public burning; 2) deleting seven other courses from the curriculum, including "Gothic Literature," "Black Literature," "Science Fiction," "Folklore and Legends," and "Whatever Happened to Mankind?"; 3) banning four books — *Growing Up Female in America, The Stepford Wives, Go Ask Alice,* and *The Bell Jar* — from the "Women in Literature" course; 4) requiring an English teacher to excise a few pages from *Student Critic,* a book that had been taught without challenge for seven years; 5) having *Go Ask Alice* permanently checked out of the school library by an administrator; 6) failing to renew the contracts of two teachers, which the plaintiffs alleged was part of the board's censorship campaign; and 7) not following the board's established procedures for reconsideration of materials and for failing to obtain community or professional input on its decisions.

District Judge Allen Sharpe dismissed the suit because "this Court lacks jurisdiction over the subject matter" and because "the complaint does not allege a violation of constitutionally protected rights." In upholding the lower court's decision, the Seventh Circuit Court observed:

> Secondary school students certainly retain an interest in some freedom of the classroom, if only through the qualified "freedom to hear" that has lately emerged as a constitutional concept. But two factors tend to limit the relevance of "academic freedom" at the secondary school level. First, the student's right to and need for such information is bounded by the level of his or her intellectual development. A high school student's lack of the intellectual skills necessary for taking full advantage of the marketplace of ideas engenders a correspondingly greater need for direction and guidance from those better equipped by experience and reflection to make critical educational choices. Second, the importance of secondary schools in the development of intellectual faculties is only one part of a broad informative role encompassing the encouragement and nurturing of those fundamental social, political, and moral values that will permit a student to take his place in the community.[18]

In the case of *Pratt* v. *Independent School District No. 831* a school board removed a film of Shirley Jackson's well-known short story "The Lottery" as well as an accompanying discussion film. Students filed suit in district court, requesting that the films be returned. The court ordered the board to reinstate the film in its curriculum. Judge Miles Lord observed:

> Case law dictates that a school board has the broad authority to regulate school curriculum . . . . This authority, however, is limited by the first amendment to the constitution. The action of a school district in removing something from the curriculum can

not be motivated by an interest in imposing a religious or scientific orthodoxy or in eliminating a particular idea from student access.[19]

## 13. What are the parents' rights if they wish to keep their children from reading or learning something to which they are opposed?

The Supreme Court has clearly held that parents have the right "to guide the education of their children." But the state also has a legitimate interest in the schooling of its future citizens, and therefore it can compel parents to provide their children with an adequate education. When school officials and parents disagree about what is best for youngsters, the right of parents may collide with those of the state.[1] At one time, the public schools, acting as the state's agents, bowed to the wishes of parents by excusing students from courses and specific assignments. Early court cases indicated that parents had a right to excuse their children from any course offered by the schools. However, today schools generally can compel students to attend courses that are deemed "basic" or "essential for good citizenship" — even over the objections of parents. But if parents can show that a course clearly violates their religious freedom, such objections will have a better chance of being respected by the courts.[2] Thus far, however, the courts have rejected the argument that the schools have violated the religious freedom of the parents and their children by imposing the "religion" of secular humanism on their children (see question 29).

The removal of a child from a course to which a parent objects is further complicated by the courts' recognition of a student's constitutional rights independent of the parents. Another complicating factor stems from school board control over schools. As Robert O'Neil explains, "While the percentage of actual participation in school board elections varies, and is often appallingly low, citizens have the chance to vote — and when they feel strongly about curricular or other school matters, they do exercise their franchise. Thus a single parental challenge to a unit or course that has been approved by an elected board (or its appointed surrogates) is antidemocratic. The clash is inevitable even where the intervention seeks to have only a single child excused, because others may seek comparable relief and may claim unequal treatment if they are not also excused. The clash is more severe, of course, where the objecting parent seeks to have the whole unit removed from the curriculum."[3]

The argument that parents should have absolute control of the education of their children in such intimate matters as sex, family life, and procreation is a strong one. But the school argument is also a strong one. As O'Neil states, "If every parent can determine what each child will study, the control of education would become chaotic. Moreover, as schools increasingly certify the content of a diploma — for college admission, employment, and the like — the need for uniformity in the curriculum becomes greater. To have the curriculum individually determined — beyond the kinds of electives that are allowed in many secondary schools — would seriously undermine the claims for acceptance and support on which the school systems in this country depend."[4]

Clashes over parental rights have led to mixed decisions in the courts, and they will unquestionably continue to do so.

## 14. Who are the schoolbook protesters?

Your nextdoor neighbor could be a schoolbook protester. It could be anyone: the couple across the street, the elderly lady on the corner, the young man who repairs TV sets, the minister, the student who delivers the daily newspaper, a member of an organization concerned about the public schools. According to surveys of the frequency of schoolbook protests, complaints are lodged primarily by parents, but protesters also include teachers, school administrators, school librarians, students, clergymen, school board members, and special interest groups. They do not represent one particular religion or a specific political party. Their economic backgrounds and occupations are as varied and interesting as the objectionable material they find in books.

## 15. Do the schoolbook protesters live primarily in small towns?

Schoolbook protesters do not live in any particular part of the nation; they can be found in all 50 states, in large cities and in small towns, in inner-city neighborhoods and in the suburbs. A listing of recorded censorship incidents during the last 10 years shows that schoolbook protest is definitely not limited to any geographic area. Schoolbook protesters are at work everywhere as the listing below will attest. Please note that this is only a partial listing.

**Alabama:** Anniston, Huntsville, Scottsboro, Tuscaloosa, State Board of Education, State Textbook Committee

**Alaska:** Anchorage, Barrow, Fairbanks, Yakutat

**Arizona:** Benson, Gilbert, Marana, Phoenix, Prescott, St. David, Thatcher, State Legislation

**Arkansas:** Concord, Glen Rose, Homer, Hot Springs, North Little Rock, Searcy

**California:** Anaheim, Anderson, Chula Vista, Concord, Cotati, Culver City, Fresno, Hayward, Imperial Beach, Jamul, Lafayette, Livermore, Mt. Diablo, Oakland, San Diego, San Jose, San Juan, Santa Clara, Santa Rosa, Walnut Creek, Yucaipa

**Colorado:** Aurora, Boulder, Denver, Glenwood, Idaho Springs, Jefferson County, La Mesa, Pagosa Springs, Widefield, State Legislation

**Connecticut:** Bethany, Darien, Enfield, Hamden, Lebanon, Ledyard, Manchester, Simsbury, State Legislation

**Delaware:** Camden, Dover, New Castle County

**Florida:** Escambia County, Ft. Myers, Haines City, Lakeland, Lee County, Orlando, Palm Beach County, Pinellas County, Polk County, St. Petersburg, Stuart, Tallahassee, Tampa, Vero Beach

**Georgia:** Atlanta, Cobb County, Gwinnett County, Savannah, Walker County

**Hawaii:** Hawaii School Board

**Idaho:** Boise, Lewiston, Moscow, St. Anthony

**Illinois:** Barrington, Champaign, Collinsville, DuPage County, Edwardsville, Glenview, Johnston City, Mahomet, Midlothian, New Trier, Normal, Norridge, Oak Lawn, Peoria, Peru, Princeton, Schaumberg, Springfield, Spring Valley, Waukegan, Winnetka

**Indiana:** Cedar Lake, Daleville, Fort Wayne, French Lick, Goshen, Highland, Marion County, New Albany, Tell City, Warsaw, Westfield, Yorktown

**Iowa:** Atlantic, Bettendorf, Burlington, Cedar Rapids, Davenport, Des Moines, Dubuque, Elkader, Kanawha, Monticello, New Hartford, Sioux City, West Des Moines

**Kansas:** Buhler, Dodge City, Gardner, Hays, Hutchinson, Mackville, Salina, Topeka, Wichita

**Kentucky:** Frankfort, Jefferson County, Louisville, Somerset

**Louisiana:** Baton Rouge, Jefferson Parish, Lafayette, Livingston, New Orleans, Monroe, Shreveport, St. Tammany Parish

**Maine:** Bath, Baileyville, Brunswick, Caribou, Dyer Brook, New Lisbon, Sanford, York

**Maryland:** Annapolis, Anne Arundel County, Federalsburg, Frederick, Glen Burnie, Harford County, Howard County, Linthicum, Middletown, Montgomery County, Potomac, Prince Georges County, Pylesville, Rockville, Salisbury, Westminster

**Massachusetts:** Athol, Buckland, Chelsea, Dedham, Holyoke, Hopkinton, Ludlow, North Adams, Orange, Pembroke, Scituate, Townsend, Waltham

**Michigan:** Bloomfield Hills, Brighton, Detroit, Flint, Grand Blanc, Grand Ledge, Hesperia, Holland, Lapeer, Middleville, Midland, Romeo, Swartz Creek, Watervliet, Wyoming

**Minnesota:** Bloomington, Deer River, Duluth, Eden Valley, Elk River, Forest Lake, Grand Rapids, International Falls, Long Prairie, Minneapolis, Park Rapids, Pipestone, St. Anthony-New Brighton, St. Cloud, St. Paul, Sauk Rapids, South St. Paul, Zimmerman

**Mississippi:** Rankin County, Mississippi Textbook Commission, State Legislation

**Missouri:** Branson, Eldon, Hillsboro, Independence, Mehlville, Mexico, Miller, Park Hill, Raytown, Springfield

**Montana:** Billings, Helena, Libby, Missoula, Whitehall

**Nebraska:** Bellevue, Dorchester, Lincoln, Omaha, Pierce, Ravenna, Wayne

**Nevada:** Carson City, Henderson, Reno

**New Hampshire:** Candia, Claremont, Merrimack, Nashua

**New Jersey:** Bergen County, Bloomsbury, Lindenwold, Mahwah, North Bergen, Norwood, Old Bridge, Pequannock, Pompton Plains, Salem, Totowa, Trenton, Wayne

**New Mexico:** Carlsbad, Santa Fe, New Mexico State Board of Education

**New York:** Binghamton, Brockport, Brooklyn, Cornwall, East Meadow, Jericho, Hannibal, Levittown, New York City, Putnam Valley, Rochester, Syracuse, Van Etten, Vernon, White Plains, Wilson

**North Carolina:** Asheboro, Buncombe County, Cabarrus County, Clinton, Durham, Greensboro, New Hanover County, Raleigh, Randolph County, Southport, Statesville, Wayne County, Winston-Salem

**North Dakota:** Minot

**Ohio:** Akron, Albany, Columbus, Continental, Dayton, Enon, Findlay, Garfield Heights, Hamilton, Hudson, Mount Vernon, North Jackson, Oak Hills, Oberlin, Rootstown, Xenia

**Oklahoma:** Boynton, Eufaula, Miami, Tulsa, State Legislation

**Oregon:** Beaverton, Corvallis, Creswell, Eagle Point, Eugene, Gervais, Glide, Hillsboro, Lincoln County, Monroe, Philomath, Pleasant Hill, Portland, Roseburg, Sandy, Springfield, Vancouver, Willamina

**Pennsylvania:** Allentown, Brodheadsville, Emporium, Girard, Harrisburg, Philadelphia, Pittsburg, Oil City, Red Cross, Scranton, Selingsgrove, Southeastern Greene, State College, Sunbury, Warrington, York County

**Rhode Island:** Portsmouth, Providence, Richmond, Westerly, Westport, Woonsocket

**South Carolina:** Columbia, Greenville, Richland

**South Dakota:** Blunt, Onida, Pierre, Sioux Falls

**Tennessee:** Church Hill, Dayton, Kingsport, Knoxville, Manchester

**Texas:** Arlington, Austin, Del Valle, Eagle Pass, Fort Worth, Hempstead, Houston, Hurst, Olney, San Antonio, State Textbook Committee

**Utah:** Heber City, Ogden, Provo

**Vermont:** Bradford, Burlington, Chester, East Montpelier, Richford, Vergennes

**Virginia:** Arlington, Charlotte County, Chesterfield County, Christianburg, Fairfax County, Gretna, Herndon, Mathews, Warrentown, Wise County

**Washington:** Hermiston, Hockinson, Issaquah, Kent, Kitsap County, Olympia, Omak, Renton, Snoqualmie, Spokane, Sumner, Vancouver, Washougal, Yelm

**West Virginia:** Kanawha County, Mercer County, Morgantown, Richwood

**Wisconsin:** Adams, Amherst, Coleman, Elkhorn, Fond du Lac, Green Bay, Howard, Montello, Mosinee, Muskego, Nashotah, New Berlin, Oconto, Racine, Solon Springs, Stevens Point, Sun Prairie, Wales, Waukesha, Wauzeka, West Allis

**Wyoming:** Casper, Gillette, Glenrock, Jackson Hole

This list is based on incidents reported in the *Newsletter on Intellectual Freedom* of the American Library Association, annual reports of People for the American Way, and press clippings.

## 16. What do the schoolbook protesters have in common?

According to persons with whom I have talked who have experienced censorship, the schoolbook protesters who insist that books be removed from public schools seem to have these common characteristics: They are convinced that they know what is best for others to see and to read. They know what is wrong with a book whether they have read it or not. They tend to judge a book by a few specific passages rather than by the book as a whole. They lack a sense of humor.

Ken Donelson, Professor of English at Arizona State University, has written many articles about school censorship. He makes these distinctions between a censor and a teacher:

> The censor, however good and decent and sincere and religious and dedicated and patriotic, is usually supremely confident of his or her own rightness. The censor seems certain while the teacher can never be. The censor knows truth while the teacher is only trying to perceive it. The censor sometimes claims to have a direct pipeline to God and truth and right while the teacher can make no such sacrilegious assertion. The censor may claim that he knows what is good for every person while the teacher knows only that each of us must take a personal trip through this world searching for the good. The censor can afford the luxury of arrogance and omniscience while the teacher can not so pretend.[1]

## 17. What are some of the tactics of the schoolbook protesters?

The American Education Coalition, a Washington-based group of organizations that have expressed displeasure with America's public schools, has prepared a series of "action kits" for "parent activists." Action Kit #1, *Organizing an Effective Parent Group*, presents these six steps:

1. *Choose Your Battle*
   According to Action Kit #1, the newly formed group should decide on the philosophy of the group, prepare a statement of purpose, decide on a mixture of negative and positive strategies and tactics, and then decide which issues to pursue.[1]

2. *Create Your Organization*
   The Action Kit states that a "parent group starts with one person." That individual enlists friends and acquaintances from differ-

ent backgrounds, including different religions. Then the group gives itself a name, agrees on assigned responsibilities, and avoids "the creation of a formal structure."[2]

3. *Choose a Course of Action*

The Action Kit suggests that the new organization study the arguments and rhetoric of the education establishment, become familiar with the "liberal mentality" by subscribing to several "liberal newsletters or tabloids," understand what makes the decision makers (administrators, educators, and school board members) tick, apply "counter-pressure until [the decision makers] decide the way you want," and build a coalition of like-minded groups.[3]

4. *Publicity*

The Action Kit recommends the selection of a spokesperson who conducts press conferences, becomes a guest on talk shows, and engages in one-to-one encounters. If the spokesperson becomes ill, the "media event" should be cancelled.[4] The spokesperson should avoid using "buzz words." "Example: 'book burners' is a liberal buzz word, 'secular humanism' is a conservative buzz word."[5]

5. *Minor and Major Events*

A well-established group should conduct a public meeting, invite a speaker with "at least a regional reputation," invite a member of the "enemy camp" but maintain control of the meeting, invite the press, and schedule and advertise a future event.[6]

6. *Future Possibilities*

Readers are advised to send for two additional action kits: *Lobbying Your Legislators and Congressmen* and *How to Get Elected to the Schoolboard.*[7]

Several interesting suggestions are offered to parent activitist groups by Connaught Marshner in *Blackboard Tyranny:* "If you mean to circulate a rumor, don't do it on your official stationery or in the name of your group."[8] "If your group plans to be very controversial, you may not wish to put officers' names on your stationery."[9]

Mrs. Marshner suggests that an activist group might want to mount "a systematic letters-to-the-editor campaign" as the need arises. "The crucial thing here is not to give the *appearance* of an organized campaign. Personally ask different 'reliables' in your club to write a letter to the editor on a specific day on a specific aspect of the topics at issue. This is, incidentally, a good way of determining who in your club is a reliable and who is not."[10]

About using call-in shows, Mrs. Marshner writes: "If the response to your appearance is good enough, you may be invited back. You can help bolster the response without telling the host that half the people who called in were your friends. . . . When a talk show features somebody you don't agree with, quickly call up a few of your reliables and get them to listen and call in as well."[11]

Mel and Norma Gabler (see question 19) offer this advice to prospective schoolbook protesters:

> to win any school battles, you must win them in the background prior to any public meetings preferably. That is, you must convince school board members and/or administrators first, for they will almost invariably support one another in public, regardless of the issue. Many times, however, one member of the board can quietly act to remove objectionable books, programs, or films; so long as it does not break out into a "fanfare". It is vitally important to do your "homework" before you begin any "campaigns" at all.[12]

To mount "the offensive against undesirable texts," the Gablers recommend that their followers take these seven steps:

1. Learn the textbook adoption procedures in your state and district.
2. Your thorough knowledge of the textbook is your best offensive weapon.
3. It is essential to mark the objectionable passages in context.
4. Hold some of your best arguments in reserve.
5. Stay on the offensive
6. Do not expect victory overnight.
7. Consider forming groups to work together.[13]

The description of a "typical" schoolbook protest incident provides additional information on the strategies of the protesters. (See questions 31 and 32.)

## 18. What are the targets of the schoolbook protesters?

During the last 12 years, I have examined thousands of pages of criticism of schoolbooks, various teaching materials, and teaching methods; and I have concluded that there are at least 200 targets of the protesters who belong to organizations. The groups do not necessarily agree on all targets, but there is a common core of at least 50 that are shared by the New Right alone.

The 60 targets that follow are among the most common found in the literature of protesting groups from either the right or the left:

1. Secular humanism. Many of the protesting organizations have identified "objectionable" materials that they maintain promote the tenets of the religion of secular humanism. Attempting to remove secular humanism from the public schools has become the number one goal of such organizations. They seem to believe that if they could convince the schools and the courts to prohibit the spreading of humanism, which they intentionally confuse with secular humanism, they could eliminate such "evils" as sex education, drug education, values clarification, evolution, and the "look-say" method of reading, among others (see questions 25 to 29 for more information on secular humanism).

2. Sex education. Norma and Mel Gabler and other schoolbook protesters call sex education "how-to courses" that are responsible for teenage pregnancies and the spreading of social diseases. The protesters maintain that a majority of parents are opposed to sex education courses in the schools despite the fact that public opinion polls show that at least 70% of Americans polled endorse such courses.

3. Drug education. The founder of a protest organization in Minnesota claims that drug education was never designed as a preventative; instead, it teaches students how to "use drugs in a responsible manner" and intensifies their desire to experiment with drugs.

4. Values clarification. The Gablers and others maintain that such courses are designed to challenge and to destroy home-taught values. The protesters maintain that values clarification courses rely on situation ethics, which, they believe, is the hallmark of secular humanism.

5. Soviet propaganda. In a speech on the Capitol steps in Washington, D.C., in which he launched a new phase of his Clean Up America

campaign, the Rev. Jerry Falwell, founder of the Moral Majority, declared that most public school textbooks are nothing more than "Soviet propaganda." He said, "Our children are being trained to deny their 200-year heritage." He then urged his followers to "rise up in arms to throw out every textbook [that seeks to deny children that heritage]."

6. Citizenship. According to Parents of Minnesota, a protesting organization, a parent should not be misled "when your child is having a course on citizenship. These are not citizenship classes as we know them to be. The new courses are designed to transfer loyalties of the child from CAPITALISM (Free Enterprise) to SOCIALISM. Socialism (according to Marxist theory) is a stage of society in transition between CAPITALISM and COMMUNISM."

7. Evolution. Members of some fundamentalist religions oppose any mention of evolution — in science and social studies textbooks as well as in novels and short stories — without an equal mention of creationism.

8. Novels, stories, poems, or plays that portray conflicts between children and their parents or between children and persons in authority. Also, literary works in which children question the decisions or wisdom of their elders.

9. Literary works that contain profanity or any "questionable" language.

10. Literary works that contain characters who do not speak standard English. Such characters, it is alleged, are designed by the authors to teach students "bad English."

11. Black literature and black dialect.

12. Literary works and textbooks that portray women in nontraditional roles (anything other than housewife and mother). On the other hand, some feminist groups object to illustrations in basal readers and other textbooks that show women in the so-called traditional roles.

13. Mythology — particularly if the myths include stories of creation.

14. Stories about any pagan cultures and lifestyles.

15. Stories about the supernatural, the occult, magic, witchcraft, Halloween, etc.

16. Ethnic studies. (One protesting organization calls ethnic studies "un-American.")

17. Violence.

18. Passages that describe sexual acts explicitly, or passages that refer to the sex act.

19. Invasions of privacy. Any questions, theme assignments, or homework that ask students to examine their personal backgrounds — family, education, religion, childhood experiences, etc. In addition, any questionnaires or assignments that allegedly violate the privacy of the family.

20. An abundance of pictures, cartoons, drawings, and songs in basal readers or in any textbooks.

21. Literature written by homosexuals; literature written about homosexuals; any "favorable" treatment of homosexuals.

22. Books and stories that do not champion the work ethic.

23. Books and stories that do not promote patriotism.

24. Negative statements about parents, about persons in authority, about the United States, about American traditions.

25. Science fiction. One protester refers to all science fiction as the "Godless books."

26. Works of "questionable writers" such as Langston Hughes, Dick Gregory, Richard Wright, Malcolm X, Eldridge Cleaver, Joan Baez, and Ogden Nash.

27. "Trash." Examples: *The Catcher in the Rye, Go Ask Alice, Flowers for Algernon, Black Boy, Native Son, Manchild in the Promised Land, The Learning Tree, Black Like Me, Daddy Was a Numbers Runner,* and *Soul on Ice.*

28. Any books or stories that do not portray the family unit (non-divorced mother and father with several children) as the basis of American life.

29. Assignments that lead the students to self-awareness and self-understanding.

30. Critical thinking skills.

31. Books and stories that contain words that disparage any individual or group — even if the language is a vital part of the dialogue that helps delineate a particular character.

32. Death education. In *Change Agents in the Schools*, Barbara M. Morris alleges that death education courses remove the fear of dying and make it easier for students to accept suicide, abortion, and euthanasia. She notes that in such courses students are taught that the "ulti-

mate, the very ultimate use of the human body is a food for other humans." She notes several selections that students allegedly read in death education courses and adds: "Students also read Jonathan Swift's *A Modest Proposal* which extolls the delights of dining on well fed babies."

33. World geography, if there is mention of "one worldism."

34. Histories that mention the United Nations.

35. Histories that point out any weaknesses in the founders of this nation or in any of the nation's leaders.

36. Uncaptioned pictures in history textbooks or in any textbooks.

37. Revisionist histories.

38. Histories that refer to this nation as a democracy instead of as a republic.

39. Ecology. One of the Gablers' employees who helps write reviews of history textbooks objects to publishers devoting "so much space to a movement that's just picking up — and that some forces are trying to push. There are plenty of people who are opposed to the ecology movement. Actually only one side has been presented — and that's usually the pro-ecology side."

40. Pollution. One protesting group objects to any mention of pollution in textbooks since the results of pollution have not been thoroughly proved and since the eradication of pollution is an "affront" to the free-enterprise system.

41. Psycho-drama and role playing.

42. Sensitivity training.

43. Behavior modification.

44. Magic circles.

45. Any psychological or psychiatric method practiced in the public schools. Any psychological principle used in teaching.

46. Assignments that ask students to make value judgments or assigned literature that prompts students to question value judgments made by others.

47. Human development and family development programs usually taught in home economics classes.

48. News magazines that publish stories about the harsh realities of life — war, crime, death, violence, and sex.

49. Magazines that contain advertisements for alcoholic beverages, birth control devices, or trips to countries like Cuba.

50. Nudity. Example: parents and school administrators have objected to the drawing of the naked boy in Maurice Sendak's *In the Night Kitchen* and to reproductions of paintings accompanying myths that show half-clad gods and goddesses.

51. Near nudity. Many copies of the annual swimwear issue of *Sports Illustrated* never reach the magazine racks in school libraries.

52. "Depressing thoughts." Example: Norma and Mel Gabler objected to the inclusion, in a basal reader, of P.T. Barnum's statement, "There's a sucker born every minute," because it's a "depressing thought."

53. Distorted content. Example: one of the Gablers' volunteer reviewers objected to a story in a basal reader because she contended that the "text is trying to stress change as being the major thing in life. This is not true. Change has no reliability; it cause [sic] the personality to be shattered."

54. Books or stories with suggestive titles. Examples: *Making It with Mademoiselle* (a book on dressmaking) and *Belly Button Defense* (a book about basketball).

55. Negative thinking. The Gablers urge their reviewers to look for examples of negative thinking in textbooks. Such thinking, according to the Gablers, includes stories about alienation, statements from members of minority groups that indicate they feel people are prejudiced against them, stories that are frightening or horrifying, stories that are depressing.

56. Isms fostered. In the outline for reviewers, the Gablers encourage their volunteers to look for favorable comments about any of the isms: communism, socialism, internationalism, and so forth. In one of their volumes of objections about textbooks submitted for adoption in Texas, the Gablers objected to a favorable mention of UNICEF in a basal reader "because it is a known Communist front."

57. Sexist and racist stereotypes.

58. The generic use of masculine pronouns when the referent may be either male or female.

59. Books in which stories or illustrations have a disproportionate number of male, white, and middle-class people.

60. Any program developed with federal funds.

## 19. Who are the Gablers and how do they affect textbooks that are used throughout the nation?

Since 1961 Norma and Mel Gabler have dedicated themselves to the task of "cleaning up" the nation's textbooks because they are convinced that textbooks exert tremendous influence on children. That belief is reflected in these two statements that seem to be the creed of their nonprofit, tax-exempt organization called Educational Research Analysts:

> Until texts are changed we must expect a continuation of the present epidemic of promiscuity, unwanted pregnancies, VD, crime, violence, vandalism, rebellion, etc.[1]

> TEXTBOOKS mold NATIONS because textbooks largely determine HOW a nation votes, WHAT it becomes and WHERE it goes![2]

Since the Gablers started reviewing textbooks and protesting what they consider to be objectionable content, their efforts have paid dividends. For example, in one of the printed sheets they distributed to their followers in 1977, they noted that "last year God gave parents a number of victories. In Texas alone, the State Textbook Committee did a good job of selecting the best of the available books. Then, the State Commissioner of Education removed 10 books, including the dictionaries with vulgar language and unreasonable definitions."[3]

One year later the Gablers sent this report to their followers:

> We submitted 659 pages in our Bills of Particulars against twenty-eight textbooks, including Supplemental Readers, Literatures, and American Histories. All of the Readers and Literature books were either oriented toward violence, cruelty, death and despair, or they were trivial. The history texts were distorted and biased against traditional American values. God saw fit to direct the State Textbook Committee to remove eighteen of these objectionable textbooks in the first stage. *Many* others should have been eliminated.[4]

In that same report the Gablers noted that the Texas State Board of Education directed the removal of Shirley Jackson's "The Lottery" from three textbooks, and it eliminated "Mateo Falcone" and "A Summer Tragedy" from one text. The Gablers had objected to all three stories.

The Gabler influence on textbooks is immeasurable. In a 1980 interview on *Donahue*, the Gablers said their reviews of textbooks were used in all 50 states and in 25 foreign countries. On that program they admitted that they review textbooks line by line, searching for material that does not coincide with their religious and political points of view. Some of us who study censorship are also convinced that the Gablers also search for anything that does not coincide perfectly with their particular view of reality or with their perception of any subject matter.

As I read about and study schoolbook protest incidents, I frequently find that the local protesters have been guided by the Gablers' reviews and strategies. And in four censorship incidents in Indiana that I personally investigated, the Gablers' reviews, strategies, and attack on secular humanism were used in each one (see question 31).

The Gablers work tirelessly at what they call their faith ministry. Perhaps the title of an article about them in *Texas Monthly* best summarizes their dedication: "The Guardians Who Slumbereth Not." They keep a schedule that few could match: "travel to meetings, consultations, and speaking engagements that takes them away from Longview more than two hundred days a year."[5] In the remainder of that time, they work with a paid staff of eight to ten and a host of volunteer reviewers, meticulously examining the books submitted for adoption in Texas.

They have become celebrities who have been featured on *60 Minutes, Donahue, Today, Nightline, Good Morning America, Freedom Report, The David Frost Show,* syndicated religious broadcasts, and numerous local radio and television talk shows.[6] James C. Hefley described their textbook crusade in *Textbooks on Trial* (Wheaton, Ill.: Victor Books, 1976), which is in its fourth printing and which has been released in paperback under the title, *Are Textbooks Harming Your Children?*

Accompanying the *Texas Monthly* article on the Gablers was a page of Gabler quotations titled "The World According to the Gablers: Ruminations from God's Angry Couple."[7] Six of those quotations follow:

> On independent thought — "Too many textbooks leave students to make up their own minds about things."

On teaching about the great depression — "It will only succeed in raising doubts about our system."

On schools today — "Crime, violence, immorality and illiteracy...the seeds of decadence are being taught universally in schools."

On peer pressure — "Any time you have a composite of a group of kids, the result is never up. It is always down."

On their own work — "What we're fighting is mental child abuse."

On modern math — "When a student reads in a math book that there are no absolutes, every value he's been taught is destroyed. And the next thing you know, the student turns to crime and drugs."

During the last 10 years, I have read hundreds of pages of objections to textbooks that the Gablers have included in the Bills of Particulars they submit to the Texas Commissioner of Education each year. The following are objections that I consider to be typical. I have provided the title of the book, the page number, the passage the Gablers object to, and then their objection as recorded in their Bill of Particulars.

*Serendipity* (a reader for grade 7)[8]
p. 67, "...the white sailors often got so drunk that they cracked the bows of ships..."
*Objection:* Since this story was written in the first person by a black slave this statement shows whites in a bad light.

p. 69, "Trusting in His (God's) goodness and justice allowed me a blind belief that one day I would be free....Why did God tolerate such treatment of black men? White men left England as men and after a few years in the island turned into monsters. Why?"
*Objection:* Insinuates that God was unjust in letting him be taken as a slave and that He should have prevented bad treatment of blacks. Depreciates God.

p. 73, "That Quakers were a type of Christian, I also knew — perhaps they were Christians who were particularly honest."
*Objection:* One is either honest or dishonest. This puts Christians in a bad light.

p. 112, "Countless species became extinct long before man ever appeared on earth."

*Objection:* Infers evolution is a fact. Trilobites and dinosaurs lived side by side with man.

p. 14, "Of all mammals man is the only one whose behavior depends almost entirely on learning."

p. 114, "No animal has been able to mold its life or environment in the way man has done."

*Objection:* Man is NOT an animal.

*Homemaking Skills for Everday Living* (grades 6-8)[9]

pp. 84-85, "How would you describe a typical American family? However you would describe it, you would be wrong. There are families with children and families without children. There are families with one parent and families with two parents. There are families with one wage earner and families with two or more wage earners. There are families with stepparents and stepchildren. There are families with grandparents, aunts, uncles, and cousins."

*Objection:* We object to this description. Until sociologists and textbooks started rewriting the composition of a family, there was not controversy. To most people families still mean those who are related by blood, marriage or adoption. Of course, there are variations, but why should this textbook dwell on the diversities?

p. 86, "The nuclear family structure is well-suited to children, 5-11."

*Objection:* This statement is too weak. It should be revised to state that the nuclear family is the ideal family, or state that only a nuclear or extended family can provide the proper environment for children.

pp. 107-108, "DIVORCE"

*Objection:* Divorce and remarriage are presented as normal and acceptable.

*Living, Learning, and Caring* (homemaking, grades 6-8)[10]

p. vii, ". . . Young people begin to question ideas they learned earlier in life. They debate points of view and search for facts. . . ."

*Objection:* Infers values and rules learned as youngsters are to be questioned and disregarded.

p. 6, "In adolescence comes the feeling that you want to be different from your parents and others. You want to be 'you.' "

*Objection:* Undermining parental values they have tried to instill in their children. Breeds disrespect and rebellion against parents.

*Exploring American Citizenship* (grade 8)[11]

p. 58, ". . . Women have gained more education in professions outside the home."

*Objection:* To expect women to receive the same pay as men ignores the fact that seniority has a decided effect on salaries received. Unless women abandon their highest profession — as mothers molding young lives — there is no way they can ever achieve seniority equal to men.

p. 58, "There has been discrimination against women, too. There are more women than men in the United States. There are more women than men of voting age. Women live longer than men. . . ."

*Objection:* This is a very biased description which does not take into consideration much of what is involved.

pp. 64-65, "A shocking case of discrimination against Asians took place in World War II. The United States was at war with Japan. But loyal Americans of Japanese descent were not trusted. More than 100,000 of these Americans lived in the Far West. Our government forced them to move into special camps. Those who owned homes had to sell them. They had to take the little money they were offered for their homes and property. The camps were guarded with barbed wire. Families lived there through the entire war. Since the war, Japanese Americans have been accepted once again. Many own businesses and farms. Thousands are professional people. A large number have graduated from college. Through their talent and hard work, they have overcome much discrimination against them."

*Objection:* This is a totally biased account that should be rewritten or removed. The students deserve a fair and accurate presentation, not one that is emotionally charged. . .

The reader might be interested in the three-page outline that the Gablers provide volunteer reviewers, which lists 129 objectionable items under 10 categories.[12] As illustrative, three categories follow:

*Negative Thinking*
A. Alienation
B. Death oriented
C. Degrading
D. Depressing
E. Despairing and hopeless
F. Discontented
G. Discouraging
H. Frightening and horrifying
I. Hate inspiring
J. Lack of respect
K. Low goals
L. Morbidness
M. No striving for excellence
N. Poverty oriented
O. Prejudicial
P. Problem stressed
Q. Skeptical
R. Suicidal

*Humanism, Occult, and Other Religions Encouraged*
A. Humanism and its tenets advanced
   1. Situation ethics
     Ex: No absolutes
       No right or wrong
       Relativism
   2. Evolution
   3. Sex education (without morals equals "how to" course)
     a. Abortion encouraged
     b. Destroys modesty
     c. Homosexuality condoned
     d. Too explicit for age level
   4. International (world community, one worldism . . .)
B. Occult spawned
   1. Astrology
   2. Satanism
   3. Superstition
   4. Tarot cards
   5. Witchcraft
C. Buddhism, Islam, Existentialism, Pantheism, etc. presented favorably

*Other Important Educational Aspects*
A. Drug education (surveys reveal increase in drug use after school drug education courses.)
B. Racism
C. Respectability given non-deserving individuals

D. Women's Lib favored

E. Overpopulation (Euthanasia, Infanticide, etc.)

F. Overemphasis on ecology

G. Evolution

H. Sex education

After reading thousands of pages of reviews by the Gablers and their volunteer reviewers, I can only conclude that any mention of the items included in their outline calls for a citation as objectionable material. For example, if characters in stories in basal readers or anthologies are depressed, alienated, discouraged, hopeless, skeptical, or suicidal, they are excoriated by the Gablers.

## 20. How does the Texas textbook adoption process affect the nation's textbooks?

Spending 64 million dollars in 1982 alone,[1] the State of Texas has become the largest single consumer of textbooks in the nation. As one of 22 states that has statewide adoption,[2] the Texas State Textbook Committee, as an arm of the Texas Education Agency, approves not more than five and no less than two textbooks in specific categories each year. Obviously publishers want their books adopted because of the size of the Texas market. And that fact gives Texas a great deal of power in the textbook publishing industry.

Like California, Texas does not necessarily accept textbooks as they are presented for adoption. Rather, the Texas State Textbook Committee conducts open hearings each summer at which citizens have the right to speak out against the books submitted for adoption. Until 1983, only those persons who were opposed to textbooks could speak at the hearings.

Those who object to textbooks submit bills of particulars in which they register their objections line by line, paragraph by paragraph. At the end of the week of hearings, publishers are given a specified time in which to respond to the objections. Then the State Textbook Committee decides which books it will adopt and tells publishers what changes must be made in the books before they will be purchased.

*Education Week* reported: "Because the Texas market is so important and because it is impractical for publishers to print separate editions for use in Texas schools, some industry officials have noted that changes that are made in textbooks to be eligible for the Texas market are also included in books offered to schools throughout the country."[3]

In 1976 the State Textbook Committee rejected these five dictionaries because the petitioners who submitted bills of particulars complained that the books contained blatantly offensive words: *The American Heritage Dictionary of the English Language,* High School Edition; *The Doubleday Dictionary; The Random House College Dictionary,* Revised Edition; *Webster's New World Dictionary of the American Language,* College Edition; and *Webster's Seventh New Collegiate Dictionary.*[4] In 1981 only two companies submitted dictionaries, and they were given the same treatment they received in 1976. Only this time one of the two companies agreed to remove the "offensive" words so that its dictionary would be accepted. The other company refused, maintaining that it would preserve the integrity of its dictionary by not bowing to the wishes of a few persons who were insensitive to language.

In 1976 publishers were ordered to remove Shirley Jackson's short story, "The Lottery," from their literature anthologies.[5] That story had been included in anthologies for more than two decades before the petitioners caused its removal. And the removal for Texas removes the story for the nation since publishers maintain that they cannot afford to publish two separate editions of textbooks — one for Texas and one for the rest of the country.

In 1982 the Gablers precipitated changes in the definition of the term *family* by their bills of particulars. One textbook gave this definition: "Generally speaking a family is a group of people who live together in one house. They may or may not be related to one another." The book also contained a section titled "Nonrelated Families" that mentioned college students, young working people, and handicapped and elderly people who live together for companionship, security, and shared expenses. The Gablers called that definition "ridiculous" and said the text was "altering values and beliefs of students."[6] The Texas Commissioner of Education ordered the publishing company to replace the definition and to delete the section on "Nonrelated Families" if it wanted its books adopted in Texas. The Commissioner ordered similar changes in another textbook.

Those are only a few examples of changes for Texas that have affected the nation. Each year, the Texas Education Agency issues a proclamation, stipulating what categories of textbooks it will adopt during the year and specifying limitations. The section of the proclamation on evolution/creationism allegedly caused publishers to tone down their treatment of evolution — even in biology textbooks. Professor Gerald Skoog of Texas Tech University sent a letter to the chairman of the State Board of Education, noting that some publishers did not submit their biology textbooks for consideration in Texas during the last adoption because of the "unreasonableness" of the Texas proclamation. He said that resulted in a narrowing of the choice of textbooks for Texas. He added that "as my research on textbooks shows, the coverage of evolution in the textbooks adopted was reduced and watered down because of this section and the unreasonable rationale that supports it in this state and elsewhere. Furthermore, this section breeds and supports other types of intimidation which censors the biology teachers of this state as they teach about the history and variation of life."[7]

The part of the proclamation dealing with creationism-evolution follows:

> Textbooks that treat the theory of evolution should identify it as only one of several explanations of the origins of humankind and avoid limiting young people in their search for meanings of their human existence.
>
> (1) Textbooks presented for adoption which treat the subject of evolution substantively as explaining the historical origins of humankind shall be edited, if necessary, to clarify that the treatment is theoretical rather than factually verifiable. Furthermore, each textbook must carry a statement on an introductory page that any material on evolution included in the book is clearly presented as theory rather than fact.
>
> (2) Textbooks presented for adoption which do not treat evolution substantively as an instructional topic, but make reference to evolution, indirectly or by implication, must be

modified, if necessary, to ensure that the reference is clearly
to be a theory and not a verified fact. These books will not
need to carry a statement on the introductory page.

(3) The presentation of the theory of evolution should be done
in a manner which is not detrimental to other theories of
origin.[8]

The Texas attorney general declared the above section in the adoption proclamation to be unconstitutional and the Texas Education Agency removed it in 1984.[9]

But there are other sections in the proclamation that are equally troublesome and that have a great impact not only on textbooks in Texas but on those used throughout the nation. During an open hearing on the adoption process, I had the opportunity to testify before the Texas State Board of Education as a representative of the National Council of Teachers of English. (See question 21.) Part of my testimony follows since I think that it shows the effects of other parts of the proclamation on textbooks in general.

> If I may, I would like to point out that as a young boy I eagerly
> read about the adventures of such heroes as Davy Crockett and
> Jim Bowie, who gave their lives for Texas, and Sam Houston, who
> devoted his life to Texas. I have read novels and works of nonfic-
> tion about citizens of this state — many of whom have made sig-
> nificant contributions to this nation. And I am saddened when I
> consider that the exploits of those heroes could not be included
> in textbooks if guideline 1.4 were strictly adhered to. That guide-
> line reads: "Textbooks shall contain no material of a partisan or
> sectarian character."
>
> As you know, one definition of partisan is "a militant supporter
> of a party, cause, faction, person, or idea." Davy Crockett, Jim Bow-
> ie and Sam Houston were all "militant supporters of a cause." So
> are hundreds of other Texas heroes, writers, politicians and busi-
> ness leaders. Taken to its extreme, guideline 1.4 would eliminate
> the sayings and exploits of hundreds of Texans from textbooks.
> If it were narrowly interpreted, that guideline would prohibit the
> adoption of textbooks that discuss religion, religious movements
> in history, and the effects of religion on politics and society. Tak-
> en to its extreme — as some textbook protesters are prone to do
> with every restrictive guideline — 1.4 could lead to the adoption

of a single, concentrated approach to a subject, such as the use of a phonics-only method in reading. [I referred to the phonics-only method here since Norma and Mel Gabler, as well as other protesters, persuaded the Texas State Textbook Committee to set up a separate category — phonics only — for basal readers. The decision to have such a category greatly disturbs most reading experts.]

Another guideline, 1.7, which refers to blatantly offensive language, could lead to the elimination of statements of such prominent Americans as Lyndon B. Johnson, Harry Truman, and Richard Nixon — among others. One of the saddest events in the history of the American textbook adoption process is that guideline 1.7 has continuously led to the removal of dictionaries from the purchase list in Texas. That removal has cast this great state in the dim light of anti-intellectualism. That removal has unfortunately indicated to the rest of the nation that some educational leaders and textbook protesters in Texas do not look upon a dictionary as a great treasure and an honest record of the American English language. That removal has been scorned throughout the nation as an act that indicates a blatant disregard for the integrity of lexicography.

Other guidelines are equally troublesome. As a student of literature, I am concerned about the section on violence. Narrowly interpreted, that guideline could lead to the exclusion of the works of Shakespeare as well as the Bible, and many of the most important works in American and world literature. Great writers do not always treat violence "in the context of its cause and its consequence," as the guideline suggests. Rather, great writers create literary works of art that reflect society, that stimulate thinking, and that may elevate humankind to think rationally about all acts — violent and non-violent.

During the last ten years, I have read hundreds of pages of objections to textbooks. What has struck me as unconscionable is the fact that some protesters have called for — and have actually succeeded in having removed — lines from poetry, paragraphs from stories, and entire works from anthologies. The integrity of an artist is apparently not recognized by such acts.

I tremble when I recall that one protester called for the removal of these lines from a poem: ". . .that means that you and I could have completely different points of view and both be right." The writer of the objection noted that the lines of the poem reflected "no definite standards and represented situation ethics." The lines of that poem were not uttered first by the poet. Rather, the lines — intentionally or not — were a paraphrase of a statement made by Abraham Lincoln in his second inaugural address.

Restrictive guidelines can be used to destroy the integrity of a subject matter, can do violence to a work of art, can destroy history. I can only hope that the members of the Board will take action that will put Texas in the forefront of the states that have statewide textbook adoption by dropping all restrictive guidelines and by encouraging publishers to publish excellent textbooks that reflect the best thinking in all subject areas, that present a variety of ideas, that stimulate thinking, that demand critical thinking, and that help produce a nation of thinking, productive Americans.[10]

## 21. How has the Texas textbook adoption process been changed?

Until 1983 the Texas State Textbook Committee permitted only those persons who objected to textbooks to testify at the public hearings. But in 1983 Barbara Parker, Director of the Freedom to Learn Project of People for the American Way (PFAW), and Michael Hudson, director of PFAW's Texas office, lobbied for a review of the adoption process. The Texas State Board of Education conducted a public hearing in May at which at least 30 speakers spoke for and against the process. (I had the privilege of speaking for the National Council of Teachers of English against the system. See question 20.) As a result of that hearing and many other meetings orchestrated by PFAW, the adoption process has been changed so that people who support certain textbooks may speak at the hearings. Other changes also have been made. The elected state board will be abolished and an appointed board will take its place. The Texas legislature passed a bill that removed the power of the Texas Commissioner of Education to overrule recommendations of the Texas State Textbook Committee. And the Texas Attorney General has declared unconstitutional that section of the adoption proclamation that calls for the origins of humankind to be balanced between evolution and creationism.

Since 1961 the Gablers have been granted an increasing amount of time each year for their testimony against textbooks submitted for adoption. In 1981, for example, they were allotted more than eight hours of the week-long hearings. But in 1983, after the process was changed, the Gablers were allotted only six minutes — the same as everyone else.

## 22. Has the Moral Majority been involved in textbook protest?

The Rev. Jerry Falwell, founder of the Moral Majority, wrote an article titled "Textbooks in Public Schools: A Disgrace and Concern to America" for the 4 May 1979 issue of *Journal Champion*, a publication of his Thomas Road Baptist Church in Lynchburg, Virginia. He wrote:

> To bring charges against textbooks may sound extreme, but we should be concerned. The vast majority of Americans are the "Moral Majority." They want America to remain a great democratic society built on (1) laws, (2) the Constitution, and (3) a devotion to truth.
>
> To oppose textbooks is not the same as book burning. This is not an attempt to censor the books of our schools. But where there are mistakes, they must be corrected . . . [1]

Falwell then pointed out mistakes in textbooks by quoting Norma and Mel Gabler (see question 19). Then he observed: "Textbook writers are humanists and evolutionists." He added that when the writers approve premarital sex, they deceive young people even though the writers have good intentions. He added: "A man may have a good intention of killing a burglar who is breaking into his home, but if he accidently shoots his son who is coming home late, his good intentions cannot undo the harm." He then declared that textbooks "deceive our young people about premarital sex, about the role of the father and the mother in the home, and even about history."[2]

Only a week before that article was published, Falwell launched a new phase of his Clean Up America campaign before an estimated 15,000 Christian "activists" in Washington, D.C. In the company of five senators and two representatives who joined him on the Capitol steps, he declared that most public school textbooks are nothing more than "Soviet propaganda." He added: "In school textbooks, pornography, obscenity, vulgarity and profanity are destroying our children's moral values in the guise of 'value clarification' and 'sex education.' Our children are being trained to deny their 200-year heritage. We must rise up in arms to throw out every textbook [that seeks to deny children their American heritage]."[3]

Followers of Falwell have heeded his words well. Shortly after the presidential election of 1980, incidents of book protest rose sharply (see question 3). Reports of individuals walking into libraries and schools, demanding removal of books in the name of the Moral Majority, circulated throughout the nation. The Moral Majority of North Carolina, Inc., sent a 30-page report to its members, citing objections to a variety of schoolbooks it had targeted and denouncing the religion of secular humanism. The cover letter on the report urged readers to read the objections to the textbooks, complete the attached coupon, and mail a check to the state Moral Majority office to support the cause. The state chairman of the Moral Majority noted in that letter: "Working together we can turn this problem around and make our schools learning centers, where a high school graduate can function at a 12th grade level, where the schools support the family and are not engaged in values clarification, promotion of sexual promiscuity, secular humanism and paperback trash."[4]

In an interview published in the *Raleigh News & Observer*, H. Lamarr Mooneyham, state chairman of the North Carolina Moral Majority, said: "Our crusade is to demonstrate the presence of secular humanism in the public schools. It's a philosophical problem. The Bible is not against books, it's against humanism."[5]

According to a feature story distributed by the *Los Angeles Times* on 22 March 1981, the Rev. Jerry Falwell sent a fund-raising letter to his followers in which he attacked *Our Bodies, Ourselves*. In the letter, Falwell asked: "Do you want your children or the children of your loved ones reading this type of immoral trash? I don't know what this country is coming to when some of our schools openly teach that premarital sex is not sinful — that the moral values that you and I grew up with are outdated and backward." He then urged citizens to examine school libraries and textbooks for "immoral, anti-family and anti-American content" and to notify the Moral Majority of their discoveries.[6]

The state chairman of the Moral Majority in Illinois said that "I would think that moral-minded people might object to books that are philosophically alien to what they believe. If they have the books and feel like burning them, fine."

On 23 November 1980 the Lynchburg, Virginia, News & The Daily Advance reported:

> The human sexuality chapters of "Life and Health" were attacked in a Moral Majority fund-raising letter earlier this month.
>
> "I think it's about time that you and I, as decent Americans, put an end to this filth and perversion once and for all," Falwell said in the letter.
>
> The letter was meant to shock people into checking into their local curriculum, said Cal Thomas, Moral Majority vice president for communications. He said "Life and Health" was used as an example because it is one of the worst books being used.
>
> Thomas hasn't seen the book. The letter was prepared by a Richmond marketing firm. "We've seen enough and have enough excerpts from it to extrapolate from there," he said.[7]

A year later, Cal Thomas said that the Moral Majority is not behind any move to censor books. He claimed that "too many people confuse it with other fundamentalist religious groups." He said the Moral Majority opposes censorship.[8]

In 1983 Cal Thomas wrote Book Burning, in which he claimed that the Moral Majority was not censoring books. Instead, he charged that the liberal secularists and the librarians were censoring ideas by keeping conservative books out of public libraries and bookstores.

Few people who study the schoolbook protest movement agree with Cal Thomas and the Moral Majority about who is censoring books. The Falwell fund-raising letters, his comments on his Old Time Gospel Hour, and his incessant attacks on secular humanism, which he maintains is the religion of the public schools, give testimony to his attitude toward books with which he and the Moral Majority do not agree.

## 23. What other organizations are involved in the protest movement?

No one can say exactly how many national, state, and local organizations protest schoolbooks in America. The number changes from month to month, since some local groups are formed to protest a single book and then disband. Other groups are formed for the same reason and remain intact for years.

When I wrote *Censors in the Classroom* in 1979, I said that I could identify at least 200 national, state, and local organizations that protest schoolbooks. Immediately after the publication of the book, I learned that a professor in Minnesota had listed more than 70 schoolbook protest groups in that state alone. I received other reports that convinced me that my estimate of 200 was extremely conservative.

Given the number of national organizations with local chapters and considering the ever-increasing number of protest incidents, I would estimate that there are no fewer than 2,000 national, state, and local organizations in the nation that protest textbooks and other teaching materials — among other activities.

How large does a local group need to be in order to have an impact on the schools? I know of one group of probably not more than five members who monitor all books in one school system. The small group has a name, a letterhead, and an inordinately powerful voice for its size. When it wants to, it gets attention in the media. No one knows the size of the organization; that is kept secret. But many people in the community are well aware of its activities.

Another group of seven has kept a school system on the West Coast on the alert for several years. Firmly believing that the public schools are preaching the religion of secular humanism, that small organization makes headlines with its attack on schoolbooks and courses.

Not all protesting groups give themselves names, and some change their names frequently. Reporting on the activities of one group, an assistant superintendent wrote:

> During the yearlong siege, we never were certain of how pervasive dissatisfaction was, although the leaders of the dissent claimed they represented "the majority" of the community. Then, too, the group's name changed as the issues progressed: "Citizens Con-

cerned with Education in Sylvania" became "Citizens Concerned with Preserving Our Traditional Heritage," which in turn became the "Committee for Scientific Creationism in the Schools," which finally evolved into the "Alliance for Better Education." Despite these name changes, the groups' leadership *always was the same* — 15 or 20 individuals who formed a type of interlocking directorate. The groups' membership rose and fell according to the specific issue under discussion, but the leaders remained the same.[1]

The following is a list of nearly 100 organizations that can be identified as existing at the time of the publication of this book. In my estimation, they represent only a twentieth of the number, since organizations like Eagle Forum, Stop Textbook Censorship, Pro-Family Forum, and Moral Majority have state and local chapters or groups in every state. (An asterisk indicates a national organization.)

Allen County Education Information Committee, Inc., Fort Wayne, Indiana

Alliance for Better Education, Sylvania, Ohio

American Association for the Advancement of Atheism, San Diego, California

American Christians in Education, Culver City, California

American Humanist Association, San Francisco, California

American Education Association*

American Education Coalition* (This organization was formed in 1983 and includes these organizations: Save Our Schools, Citizens for Educational Freedom, the National Christian Action Coalition, the National Association of Evangelicals, the American Legislative Exchange Council, United Families of America, and the National Pro-Family Coalition. That is the organizational membership announced in the *Washington Times*, 2 June 1983.)

America's Future, Inc.*

American Society of Atheists*

Billy James Hargis' Christian Crusade,* Tulsa, Oklahoma

The John Birch Society*

California Monitor of Education

Centre County Chapter of Citizens Concerned for Human Life, State College, Pennsylvania

Citizens Advocating a Voice in Education (CAVE), Georgia

Christian Anti-Communism Crusade,* Long Beach, California
Citizens Coalition, Albany, New York
Citizens Committee for Excellence in Education, Walnut Creek, California
Citizens Committee of California, Inc., Fullerton, California
Citizens Committee on Education, Pinellas County, Florida
Citizens for Decency in Public Schools, Jefferson County, Kentucky
Citizens for Educational Reform*
Citizens United for Responsible Education (CURE), Montgomery County, Maryland
Colorado Committee to Upgrade Public Education (CUPE)
Committee for Positive Education, Warren, Ohio
Committee for Responsible Education, Tulsa, Oklahoma
Concerned Citizens of Elkader, Iowa
Concerned Citizens of Middletown Valley, Middletown, Maryland
Concerned Parents of Monticello, Iowa
Concerned Parents and Taxpayers for Better Education, Concord, New York
Concerned Parents and Taxpayers for Better Education, Nashua, New Hampshire
Concerned Women of America*
Council on Interracial Books for Children*
Creation-Science Research Center*
Daughters of the American Revolution*
Decatur Committee for Decency, Decatur, Texas
Decency in Education, Fort Myers, Florida
The Eagle Forum*
Educational Research Analysts*
Educational Voucher Institute*
Fair Education Foundation, Inc., Clermont, Florida
Frederick County Civic Federation, Frederick, Maryland
Freedom from Religion Foundation, Madison, Wisconsin
Guardians of Traditional Education, Bowie, Maryland
Growing Without Schooling*
Guardians of Education for Maine (GEM)
The Heritage Foundation*
Humanist Quest for Truth, Brighton, Colorado

Indiana Home Circle, Bloomington, Indiana

Informed Moral Persons Against Contrary Teaching (IMPACT), Roots-town, Ohio

Institute of American Ideals*

Ku Klux Klan (KKK)*

Learn, Inc.*

Let's Improve Today's Education,* Phoenix, Arizona

Maryland Coalition of Concerned Parents on Privacy Rights in Public Schools

The National Congress for Educational Excellence*

National Association for the Advancement of Colored People* (occasional activity by a local chapter)

National Association for Neighborhood Schools, Inc.*

National Association of Home Education*

National Organization for Women (NOW)*

Parents for Academic and Responsible Education (PARE),* Palm Beach, Florida

Parents for Basic Education, Lapeer, Michigan

Parents of Minnesota, Inc.

Parents' Rights, Inc.*

People Have a Say in Education (PHASE),* Yucaipa, California

People of America Responding to the Educational Needs of Today's Society (PARENTS), Kenosha, Wisconsin

People Who Care, Warsaw, Indiana

Posse Comitatus*

Pro-Family Forum*

Reading Reform Foundation,* Scottsdale, Arizona

Santa Clara County Citizens Action Committee Opposing Family Life Education, San Jose, California

The Society of Evangelical Agnostics, Fresno, California

Save Our Schools (SOS)*

Sequoia Institute*

Stop Textbook Censorship Committee*

Texas Society of the Daughters of the American Revolution

Tomorrow River Concerned Parents, Amherst, Wisconsin

WATCH, Linthicum, Maryland

We Love Our Children, Westfield, Indiana

Young Parents Alert, Lake Elmo, Minnesota

## 24. How are the organizations affiliated?

Shortly after it was formed, the American Education Coalition consisted of seven organizations concerned about public and private education (see question 23). The affiliation of those organizations is quite obvious; such is not the case with many other schoolbook protest organizations.

A common link to hundreds of national, state, and local organizations is provided by Norma and Mel Gabler and their Educational Research Analysts (see question 19). Writing about the Gablers in *Texas Monthly*, William Martin commented that they have become "an integral institution of the New Right, whose agenda they share almost point for point. Their work is commended by Moral Majority leader Jerry Falwell, anti-ERA activist and Eagle Forum founder Phyllis Schlafly, and New Right direct-mail expert Richard Viguerie. They participate in gatherings sponsored by such New Right organizations as the Committee for the Survival of a Free Congress and the Texas-based Pro-Family Forum."[1]

Affiliations of schoolbook protesting organizations have as much right to exist as do associations that link doctors, lawyers, teachers, or ministers. However, the affiliations should be known to school personnel who have to respond to groups that are protesting school materials. Then they will understand why so many of the protesters have the same targets, use almost identical rhetoric, and cite the same "objectionable" passages in library books and textbooks. The realization that a small, local group is affiliated with a larger organization or group of organizations should help local school officials respond to the charges and inform local citizens about the total agenda of the complaining group.

# 25. What is the religion of secular humanism?

Rev. Tim LaHaye, a California minister and one of the founders of the Moral Majority, attacks the religion of secular humanism in his best-selling books, sermons, speeches, and television appearances. In *The Battle for the Mind,* he declared: "Most of the evils of the world today can be traced to humanism, which has taken over the government, the UN, education, TV, and most of the other influential things of life."[1] In his *The Battle for the Public Schools,* LaHaye charges that humanists have invaded public classrooms, brainwashing children with ideas about evolution, sex, death, socialism, internationalism, and situation ethics. Humanists, according to LaHaye, are "secular educators who no longer make learning their primary objective. Instead our public schools have become conduits to the minds of youth, training them to be anti-God, antimoral, antifamily, anti-free enterprise, and anti-American."[2]

What is this "religion" that enrages the Moral Majority and that has led to numerous attacks on the nation's public schools, their libraries, their teachers, and their textbooks? Definitions abound. But one of the most common is distributed by Norma and Mel Gabler through their Educational Research Analysts, which they call the nation's largest textbook review clearinghouse. Part of that definition follows:

> Humanism is faith in man instead of faith in God. Humanism was officially ruled a religion by the U.S. Supreme Court. Humanism promotes: (1) situation ethics, (2) evolution, (3) sexual freedom, including public sex education courses, and (4) internationalism. . . .
>
> Humanism centers on "self" because it recognizes no higher being to which man is responsible. Thus there is much emphasis in public education on each child having a "positive self-concept." The child must see a good picture of himself. This eliminates coming to Christ for forgiveness of sin. It eliminates the Christian attributes of meekness and humility. Where does self-esteem end and arrogance begin?
>
> Such terms as self-concept, self-esteem, self-awareness, self-acceptance, self-fulfillment, self-realization, self-understanding, self-actualization, body awareness, etc. are frequently used. All leave the students occupied primarily with themselves and this is wrong.

> There are others to consider. Self-centered persons are seldom
> an asset to themselves, to their friends, family or country.[3]

That definition has been expanded several times to include more
targets of the schoolbook protesters. For example, Rev. LaHaye devotes
27 pages of his *The Battle for the Public Schools* to prove that secular
humanism has all "the markings" of a religion.[4] In that chapter and
others, he attacks these "hallmarks" of secular humanism: the look-
say method of reading, values clarification, death education, global education, evolution, sex education, total reading freedom, the "negation"
of Christianity in the schools, and socialism, among others.[5]

But regardless how much is written about secular humanism and how
many definitions are circulated, it is interesting that few persons can
define the religion of secular humanism even though they say it is cor-
rupting youth. One organizer of parent protest groups defined the religion on a national television program as "the philosophy of anything
goes."[6] Another school critic told a school board that humanism is the
"belief that if something feels good, do it." Others believe that the Supreme Court established secular humanism as the religion of the public schools when it "removed God" from classrooms in the case of
*Abington* v. *Schempp*. That belief is supported by Senator Jesse Helms,
who wrote:

> When the U.S. Supreme Court prohibited children from participat-
> ing in voluntary prayers in public schools, the conclusion is ines-
> capable that the Supreme Court not only violated the right of free
> exercise of religion of all Americans; it also established a national
> religion in the United States — the religion of secular humanism.[7]

What, then, is secular humanism? As used by the critics of the public schools, it seems to be a "buzz word" that is applied to anything
that the critics do not like and want to remove from the schools. (See
questions 26, 27, 28, and 29.)

## 26. What do the protesters hope to accomplish by proving that the schools promote the religion of secular humanism?

If the protesters succeed in taking a case to the Supreme Court in which they can prove that the public schools actually preach the religion of secular humanism, they could achieve several goals. The separation of church and state as guaranteed by the First Amendment prohibits the schools from teaching a specific religion. Therefore, if the court determines that the schools are preaching secular humanism, then they would have to stop teaching any and all of the tenets of that religion. Thus, the protesters could rid the schools of sex education, values clarification, death education, evolution, and a host of subjects and topics that they maintain are hallmarks of secular humanism.

If the Supreme Court did not order the public schools to stop teaching the subjects that might be labeled secular humanism, then the protesters could demand equal time and money for their religions to be taught in the public schools, or, more likely, they could demand federal and state money for their private schools.

## 27. What arguments do the protesters offer to substantiate their charges that the schools preach the religion of secular humanism?

Essentially the same argument is repeated in the literature of New Right organizations and in the more than 20 books they use to support the allegation that secular humanism is the religion of the public schools. Here is how it goes. John Dewey and 33 other "liberal humanists" signed *Humanist Manifesto I* in 1933. B.F. Skinner signed *Humanist Manifesto II* in 1973. Since those two prominent educators, among others, signed the documents, it follows — goes the argument — that all educators subscribe to the tenets of the manifestos, which members of the New Right call the bibles of public school teachers. Next, since there is an American Humanist Association (AHA) that publishes articles about secular humanism and its goals, it follows — goes the argument — that America's public school teachers belong to the organization and read its journals. Finally, since the Supreme Court declared secular humanism to be a religion, the spreading of the doctrine of humanism in the public schools — the argument continues — is in direct violation of the First Amendment.

## 28. What arguments can be used to refute the charge that the schools preach secular humanism?

There are at least four flaws in the argument that members of the New Right advance to prove that secular humanism is the religion of the schools. First, probably no more than 3% of the public school teachers and administrators in this nation even know about — let alone have read — either *Humanist Manifesto*.[1] Second, thousands of today's teachers know pitifully little about John Dewey and his philosophy of education. Simply because a prominent educator called himself a secular humanist, it does not follow that all who enter the teaching profession are secular humanists.

Third, the Moral Majority and other New Right organizations attribute great influence over education to the American Humanist Association (AHA), the publisher of the manifestos. But AHA has fewer than 4,000 members, and only a handful of the nation's two million teachers and administrators even know about AHA — let alone call themselves members. Fourth, the Supreme Court did not *declare* secular humanism to be a religion. In the frequently cited case of *Torcaso* v. *Watkins*, this footnote is inclued: "Among religions in this country which do not teach what would generally be considered a belief in the existence of God are Buddhism, Taoism, Ethical Culture, Secular Humanism and others."[2] In a second case that is often cited,[3] there is a footnote referring to *Torcaso*. Two footnotes hardly constitute a Supreme Court *declaration*.

But the battle over secular humanism has only begun. In June 1984 Congress passed the Education for Economic Security Act of 1984 with an amendment on magnet schools assistance that was introduced by Senator Orrin Hatch. Section 709 of that amendment reads as follows: "Grants under this title may not be used for consultants, for transportation, or for any activity which does not augment academic improvement, or for any course of instruction the substance of which the LEA [local education agency] determines is secular humanism."[4]

Referred to as the secular humanism ban, the amendment provoked protest from professional organizations that consider it to be dangerous to public school education. As noted in question 25, the schoolbook protesters who are convinced that secular humanism is the religion of the public schools have difficulty defining it. Now the LEAs must define it if they have magnet schools. The question is: Why should the LEAs define it? Why has it not been defined by the author of the amendment or by the Department of Education in its regulations? What is the purpose of the amendment? How can it be used to rid the schools of courses that the New Right opposes?

The American Civil Liberties Union called the amendment a "license for local school boards to suppress any disfavored ideas, simply by labeling those ideas 'secular humanism'."[5] In challenging the constitutionality of the amendment, the ACLU called it "an extraordinary federal intrusion into local education policy, animated by hostility to basic First Amendment values of tolerance, open-mindedness, and religious neutrality."[6] As this book was going to press in November 1985, Congress dropped the 16-word secular humanism clause from the amendment.

## 29. How have the courts responded to the charge that the public schools preach secular humanism?

Federal courts in the states of Washington and Tennessee have considered the secular humanism charge during the last three years. In both cases, the plaintiffs accused the schools of indoctrinating children with the religion of secular humanism through books that were used in different classes. In both cases, the judges in the trial courts dismissed the suits on the grounds that insufficient evidence had been presented to back the charges.

In *Grove* v. *Mead*, Michael Farris, the former president of the Moral Majority in the state of Washington, sued a school district for refusing to remove Gordon Parks' *The Learning Tree* from the curriculum. Farris, who is an attorney, charged that when the school system refused to remove the book, it violated students' First Amendment rights by imposing on them the religion of secular humanism.[1] The circuit court of appeals upheld the lower court's decision, and Farris has appealed the decision to the Supreme Court, which has not yet acted on the case.

Michael Farris also was involved in the second suit — this time in Tennessee. Acting as the attorney for Beverly LaHaye's Concerned Women for America, Farris filed a brief for a case that began in Church Hill, Tennessee. In *Mozert et al.* v. *Hawkins County Public Schools*, the parents of children in elementary and junior high schools alleged that the First Amendment rights of their children were violated when they were forced to study secular humanism as presented in the Holt, Rinehart & Winston basal readers.[2] After the trial court dismissed the suit, Farris appealed to the circuit court of appeals, which has remanded the case to the lower court for trial in March 1986.

## 30. What is the Hatch Amendment and what does it have to do with the schoolbook protest movement?

The Hatch Amendment on psychological testing became part of Public Law 95-561 on 1 November 1978. The amendment follows:

### Protection of Pupil Rights

(a) All instructional material, including teacher's manuals, films, tapes, or other supplementary instructional material which will be used in connection with any research or experimental program or project shall be available for inspection by the parents or guardians of the children engaged in such program or project. For the purpose of this section "research or experimentation program or project" means any program or project in any applicable program designed to explore or develop new or unproven teaching methods or techniques.

(b) No student shall be required, as part of any applicable program, to submit to psychiatric examination, testing, or treatment, or psychological examination, testing, or treatment, in which the primary purpose is to reveal information concerning:

    (1) political affiliations;

    (2) mental and psychological problems potentially embarrassing to the student or his family;

    (3) sex behavior and attitudes;

    (4) illegal, anti-social, self-incriminating and demeaning behavior;

    (5) critical appraisals of other individuals with whom respondents have close family relationships;

    (6) legally recognized privileged and analogous relationships, such as those of lawyers, physicians, and ministers, or

    (7) income (other than that required by law to determine eligibility for participation in a program or for receiving financial assistance under such program), without prior consent of the student (if the student is an adult or emancipated minor), or in the case of unemancipated minor, without the prior written consent of the parent.

Little attention was paid to the amendment until Phyllis Schlafly and the Eagle Forum persuaded the Department of Education to conduct a series of public hearings on it in 1984. The hearings led to the implementation orders in November 1984 as well as to the publication of Schlafly's *Child Abuse in the Classroom*, which consists of excerpts from "official transcripts" of the hearings.

Two months after the implementation order, the Eagle Forum published a copy of a letter to school board presidents prepared by the Maryland Coalition of Concerned Parents on Privacy Rights in Public Schools. By February 1985 the letter had been submitted to school boards by parents in 17 states who thought the Hatch Amendment applied to classroom activities as well as to psychological testing. The letter is reprinted here as it appeared in *The Eagle Forum Newsletter:*

PARENTS; HOW TO PROTECT YOUR RIGHTS — Here is a sample letter which you can copy and send to the president of your local School Board (with copy to your child's school principal) in order to protect parental and student rights under the Hatch Amendment Regulations effective Nov. 12, 1984. This letter does not ask for the removal of any course or material;

it merely demands that the school obey the law and secure written parental consent before subjecting children to any of the following. Parents are NOT required to explain their reasons for denying consent.

Date:

To: School Board President

Dear        :

I am the parent of                who attends            School. Under U.S. legislation and court decisions, parents have the primary responsibility for their children's education, and pupils have certain rights which the schools may not deny. Parents have the right to assure that their children's beliefs and moral values are not undermined by the schools. Pupils have the right to have and to hold their values and moral standards without direct or indirect manipulation by the schools through curricula, textbooks, audio-visual materials, or supplementary assignments.

Accordingly, I hereby request that my child be involved in NO school activities or materials listed below unless I have first reviewed all the relevant materials and have given my written consent for their use:

Psychological and psychiatric examinations, tests, or surveys that are designed to elicit information about attitudes, habits, traits, opinions, beliefs, or feelings of an individual or group;

Psychological and psychiatric treatment that is designed to affect behavioral, emotional, or attitudinal characteristics of an individual or group;

Values clarification, use of moral dilemmas, discussion of religious or moral standards, role-playing or open-ended discussions of situations involving moral issues, and survival games including life/death decision exercises;

Death education, including abortion, euthanasia, suicide, use of violence, and discussions of death and dying;

Curricula pertaining to alcohol and drugs;

Instruction in nuclear war, nuclear policy, and nuclear classroom games;

Anti-nationalistic, one-world government or globalism curricula;

Discussion and testing on inter-personal relationships; discussions of attitudes towards parents and parenting;

Education in human sexuality, including pre-marital sex, extra-marital sex, contraception, abortion, homosexuality, group sex and marriages, prostitution, incest, masturbation, bestiality, divorce, population control, and roles of males and females; sex behavior and attitudes of student and family;

Pornography and any materials containing profanity and/or sexual explicitness;

Guided fantasy techniques; hypnotic techniques; imagery and suggestology;

Organic evolution, including the idea that man has developed from previous or lower types of living things;

Discussions of witchcraft, occultism, the supernatural, and Eastern mysticism;

Political affiliations and beliefs of student and family; personal religious beliefs and practices;

Mental and psychological problems and self-incriminating behavior potentially embarrassing to the student or family;

Critical appraisals of other individuals with whom the child has family relationships;

Legally recognized privileged and analogous relationships, such as those of lawyers, physicians, and ministers;

Income, including the student's role in family activities and finances;

Non-academic personality traits; questionnaires on personal and family life and attitudes;

Autobiography assignments; log books, diaries, and personal journals;

Contrived incidents for self-revelation; sensitivity training, group encounter sessions, talk-ins, magic circle techniques, self-evaluation and auto-criticism; strategies designed for self-disclosure (e.g., zig-zag);

Sociograms, sociodrama; psychodrama; blindfold walks; isolation techniques.

The purpose of this letter is to preserve my child's rights under the Protection of Pupil Rights Amendment (the Hatch Amendment) to the General Education Provisions Act, and under its regulations as published in the *Federal Register* of Sept. 6, 1984, which became effective Nov. 12, 1984. These regulations provide a procedure for filing complaints first at the local level, and then with the U.S. Department of Education. If a voluntary remedy fails, federal funds can be withdrawn from those in violation of the law. I respectfully ask you to send me a substantive response to this letter attaching a copy of your policy statement and procedures for parental permission requirements, to notify all my child's teachers, and to keep a copy of this letter in my child's permanent file. Thank you for your cooperation.

copy to School Principal                    Sincerely,

Shortly after the regulations had been published and after the aforementioned letter had been distributed in a number of states, Senator

Orrin Hatch, author of the Hatch Amendment, attempted to clarify the intent of his act in a speech on the Senate floor. He said that he was "amazed at the overreaction of educational lobby groups to the [Education] Department's regulations."[1]

Directing part of his remarks to such groups as Phyllis Schlafly's Eagle Forum, Senator Hatch said:

> some parent groups have interpreted both the statute and the regulations so broadly that they would have them apply to all curriculum materials, library books, teacher guides, et cetera, paid for with State or local money. They would have all tests used by teachers in such non-federally funded courses as physical education, health, sociology, literature, et cetera, reviewed by parents before they could be administered to students. Because there are no Federal funds in such courses, the Hatch amendment is not applicable to them. A number of states do, however, have statutes or State board regulations which do safeguard these parental rights.
>
> Some other parent groups contend that because school districts receive some Federal funds on a formula basis such as impact aid, Chapter I, et cetera, when a teacher made test is given that may ask such pupils to make a value judgment on a topic, this would invoke the Hatch amendment. This was never the intent of the Hatch amendment.
>
> Were a school district to use its Chapter II funds to establish experimental, demonstration or testing programs, the primary purpose of which is to elicit the type of information proscribed by the Hatch amendment, that activity would fall within the purview of the amendment. A direct relationship can be determined, and Federal funds would be paying for an activity that could be challenged under the Department of Education regulations.
>
> On the other hand . . . if the Chapter II funds were used to pay for a course in citizenship — as authorized by Chapter II — and the local school board agrees to allow a political science graduate student whose dissertation project is funded from non-Federal sources to administer a survey — which is actually a test — to the class, and that survey attempts to elicit information about the student's perceptions of politics, politicians, people who work for governments, and so forth, because such questions may cause a student to divulge his or her — or their parent's — political persuasion, a parent may ask to have their child excused, but if re-

fused, the relief, it would seem to me, would have to be on some basis other than the Hatch amendment.

. . . there are also those who would have certain courses, such as sex education, paid for with other than Federal funds, eliminated from the curriculum. They contend that the Hatch amendment prevails because in such courses, pupils cannot discuss the course content without making some value judgments about sexual behavior. Were such a course to be funded with Chapter II funds, for example, it certainly would be covered by the Hatch amendment and the Department of Education regulations. If the course is nonfederally funded, the Hatch amendment does not prevail.[2]

Senator Hatch said that the purpose of the amendment was "to guarantee the right of parents to have their children excused from federally funded activities under carefully specified circumstances." The "activities we are talking about are non-scholastic in nature."[3]

At the beginning of the 1985-86 academic year, the letter distributed by the Eagle Forum was being used by parents in several dozen states and in at least one Department of Defense school in Germany. The confusion over the amendment continued with the same question being asked throughout the nation: Which is actually the amendment — what was passed in the Senate or what was published in the letter distributed by the Eagle Forum? The answer to that question should be obvious. Unfortunately, members of the Eagle Forum and other protesting groups do not recognize the obvious answer. Consequently, the amendment is being used in an attempt to rid the schools of courses, teaching materials, and teaching methods that were apparently not the target of Senator Hatch when he drafted the amendment.

## 31. What is the censorship tale of Tell City, and is it a typical incident?

Tell City, Indiana, experienced a winter of discontent in 1982 when two ministers and some of their followers accused the school system of teaching the religion of secular humanism. Probably no more than 20 citizens in the southern Indiana town had heard of the so-called religion of the public schools before the charge was made, and probably no more than that can define the religion now. But hundreds of Tell City's citizens will not soon forget the phrase; the vehemence with which it was hurled at the school board, teachers, and administrators; and the wounds that are slow to heal from the battle over the secular humanism charge.

When a ninth-grade student showed his mother a few passages in John Steinbeck's *Of Mice and Men*, he told her that he did not want to read the book as part of his class assignment. After hearing the complaint of the mother, the English teacher who had assigned the novel told the mother that her son could read Stephen Crane's *Red Badge of Courage* as independent reading while the rest of the class read Steinbeck. The mother and her son apparently accepted the alternate assignment, and later she even told the media that she and her son had been treated well by the teacher. But the mother also talked with her minister about the novel, and he expressed his displeasure with the assignment, with the Tell City schools in general, and with the English department in the high school in particular.[1]

The Rev. Don Reynolds, pastor of the Abundant Life Church, had just opened a Christian academy in Tell City. He told his congregation and at least one other minister about the "evil" novel. The two ministers prepared a petition to be presented to the school board; and at the January meeting, a group of 10 demanded that books "containing profanity and suggestive remarks" not be used in the schools. Then the minister from nearby Hawesville, Kentucky, who was acting as spokesperson for the group, accused the school board of being "anti-God." That evening marked the beginning of a three-month schoolbook protest that brought television cameras, nationally prominent textbook protesters, and divisiveness to the town nestled in the bend of the Ohio River.

Shortly after the mother asked for the alternate assignment, members of the Tell City School Board discovered that they had never formally adopted their four-year-old policy for handling complaints about teaching materials. So the five-member board voted unanimously to make the policy official.

No one in Tell City, Indiana — nor the minister from Hawesville, Kentucky — completed a complaint form calling for a review of Steinbeck's *Of Mice and Men*. Nor did anyone sign a complaint form about *Finding My Way*, a textbook used in an elective sex education course for seventh and eighth grades. Instead, a small group led by a minister from a neighboring state protested the teaching of both books at the January meeting of the school board and used the local radio station and newspaper to condemn the books and the school system.

The minister from Kentucky presented the Tell City School Board with a petition signed by approximately 60 persons. The Rev. Steve Epley charged that the ninth-grader was "required" to read *Of Mice and Men*. The minister then read this statement from a letter attached to the petition:

> When he refused to read the book, he was barred from English class and forced to spend the entire period in a small room by himself with a thicker book and no assistance from his teacher. We ask your help in our fight to clean up the garbage in Tell City High School's English department. We, as Christians, need to take a stand against Satan's attack upon the minds of our youth.

Answering the charges during the board meeting, Robert Waters, the ninth-grader's English teacher, said that no student in the high school is ever "required" to read a given novel or play and that the boy was assigned to read *The Red Badge of Courage* on his own in the English office during regular class time. Waters said the "small room" the Rev. Epley referred to is an English resource room that is about half the size of a conventional classroom.

Several days after the January meeting of the board, the Rev. Epley, writing a guest column for the *Tell City News*, raised the specter of secular humanism with these words:

> I am very much concerned about the humanist teachings in our public schools.

> What is Humanism? It is religion without God. It is education without God. It is the condition of man as described in the Bible (Romans 1:28) ". . . they did not like to retain God in their knowledge . . ." and the results are indeed tragic.
>
> The Humanist is more dangerous than the atheist. At least, an atheist will come right out and say he doesn't believe in God. A humanist will say, "Yes, I believe there is a God, but . . . I also believe in evolution."
>
> The atheist is like a rattlesnake. He will make some noises before he bites you. But the Humanist is more like a boa constrictor. He will silently squeeze you to death with his Godless philosophies before you know what happened.

With those words, Tell City's teachers joined the ranks of thousands who have been charged with "preaching the religion of secular humanism" in the public schools. And like the thousands who have been so charged, Tell City's teachers were unaware of the crimes they were allegedly committing against society. They did not attend a church called Secular Humanist — in fact, they could not find one in Indiana if they tried. They could not define the religion, nor could they state its major beliefs. Yet they stood accused of spreading some ill-defined doctrine that their accusers could not define and that prompted one minister in Tell City to call them "pagans and heathens" on a radio program. Another minister called school board members and the superintendent "rotten, stinking hypocrites who are spreading the religion of humanism through sex education."

Not all of the ministers in Tell City thought the schools were teaching secular humanism. Early in the controversy, three Catholic priests and four Protestant ministers sent a joint letter to the superintendent, expressing their support for the school system. Several civic groups and organizations did the same.

Shortly after the Rev. Epley denounced the humanists in Tell City, a small group of citizens began compiling objections to some of the materials used in the public schools. At the February meeting of the school board, the Rev. Reynolds condemned the school system for allowing students to play *Dungeons & Dragons* in classrooms. He questioned the educational value of the game and made reference to the Supreme Court ruling that no longer permits prayer in public schools. "And yet this game teaches children to pray to gods and they will receive power . . . magical power by praying to these gods," the minister said. He then showed the school board a picture which he said came from a book written by the founder of the First Church of Satan. The minister said that the picture "shows a nude lady lying on an altar, and this is part of their ritual as they worship Satan. You will find in one of the *D&D [Dungeons & Dragons]* manuals a picture of the same altar with the same thing happening."

The minister then expressed his fear that if children are exposed to such material in the game manual, "they will pursue the interest and eventually wind up with the same pornography. We look at the picture in the book and it shows nude women, which according to the Supreme Court is classified as pornography, and if that's acceptable in our public school classrooms, then something's wrong."

Several students took issue with the minister's statements. In an interview published in the *Tell City News*, one student was quoted as having said: "The basic premise of the game is to overcome evil. It seems to me the minister was confused. He was confusing what the characters do in the game as opposed to what people do. He made some comments that were not entirely true . . . I heard him tell somebody that he only bought the manual [a handbook for *Dungeons & Dragons*] that night. I think if he understood the game better, he would have no grounds to be opposed to it."

Throughout the schoolbook controversy in Tell City, Superintendent William Wilson patiently explained that *Dungeons & Dragons* is played in a non-credit mini-course by students who elect the class. He also pointed out that no picture of a nude woman appears anywhere in the manual that accompanies the game. He further explained — again and again throughout the protest — that no students are forced to take sex education; rather, they elect to take it and they must have parental permission to do so.

On February 16, the Rev. Reynolds announced that Norma and Mel Gabler would appear at a rally at the National Guard Armory in Tell City at the end of the month (see question 19). Illness forced Norma to stay at home in Longview, Texas; consequently, Mel was the principal speaker.

Approximately 300 persons, including the chairperson of Phyllis Schlafly's Stop Textbook Censorship Committee, attended the rally.

Reporters estimated that at least one-third of the audience was there to show support of the school system.

In his speech, Mel Gabler attacked the religion of secular humanism, sex education, *Dungeons & Dragons*, and textbooks in general. He cited many passages in textbooks — only one of which was used in Tell City — to reinforce his belief that many of today's textbooks are dangerous because they promote evolution as unquestioned scientific fact, situation ethics, sex education, world citizenship, and socialism — all of which he believes are tenets of the religion of secular humanism.

Shortly after Mel Gabler noted that students in Tell City are forced to take sex education, he had to retract that statement when he was informed that sex education is an elective course. But he did accuse the school system of teaching "frills not skills," and he stated emphatically that standardized test scores in Tell City had declined steadily.

The superintendent, school board members, teachers, and administrators refuted the charges of Mel Gabler and others during the March meeting of the school board. Test scores have risen — not declined — the audience was told, and evidence was offered to support that statement. The basics are stressed in regular academic courses; *Dungeons & Dragons* is played only in a non-credit, elective mini-course. The school authorities repeated again and again: no student is required to take sex education; parental consent is required before a student may take the elective course.

At the beginning of the March meeting of the board, Superintendent Wilson explained that the entire meeting would be devoted to the charges made during the January and February board meetings, as well as to the allegations made on radio programs, in newspapers, and at the rally. At the conclusion of the three-hour session, Anthony Pappano, president of the school board, read a statement in which he charged that the protesters used questionable tactics to protest the books. According to Pappano, the school critics did not follow the procedures for objecting to books; rather, he charged that the critics used the mass media and the rally to distort the truth and to make false and libelous statements. He promised that future school board meetings would not be used "as a forum by self-righteous groups to promote their personal beliefs. There will be no further discussion by the board on the topic of censorship until all interested parties have followed the established procedures of this school corporation." Finally, Pappano warned that if the protesting group persisted in using its present tactics and if it continued to make false and libelous statements about the school system and its employees, "we are prepared to take any and all legal action necessary to defend the constitutional rights of individuals associated with this corporation, including the educational rights of our children."

The Rev. Reynolds scheduled no further rallies as he had promised. He did not bring Norma Gabler, Phyllis Schlafly, and Billy O'Hair to Tell City. Rather, he closed his Christian academy and left the community. The teachers, administrators, and school board members returned to the task of providing a solid education for the students in the community. But the events of the winter of 1982 have not been forgotten, and the scars are slow to heal.

The schoolbook protest at Tell City contains many of the ingredients common to incidents elsewhere in the country. It is not unusual to find at least half — if not all — of the following in organized protests:

1. One book frequently precipitates a protest, but it does not take long for other books, courses, or activities to be added.
2. Most of the protesters have not read the entire works they find objectionable. Rather, they take sentences out of context, rely on the objections of others, and frequently distort facts.
3. The protesters do not always follow established procedures in protesting books and courses; rather, they put the questionable materials on trial in the mass media.
4. The charge that the school system is preaching the religion of secular humanism is spread by the protesters, but few can define the religion and substantiate the charges.
5. Like the rest of the community, the clergy becomes divided, with part joining the protesters and with others supporting the schools.
6. Outsiders are brought in to support the protesters.
7. The community is divided.

# 32. What can be learned from the Tell City incident?

- Every school system should have a set of procedures for handling complaints about books and other teaching materials, and those procedures should be followed assiduously.

- Every school system should have a materials selection policy that covers the selection of textbooks, library books, and all teaching materials.

- If a teacher or librarian is accused of teaching or disseminating "objectionable" material, that person should be fully apprised of the charge as soon as possible.

- The person making the charge should be encouraged to meet, in an informal session, with the teacher or librarian accused of teaching or disseminating the "questionable" material.

- Any person making a charge against the school system or against a specific book, course, teaching method, and so on, should be given a fair and courteous hearing.

- The school board and school administrators have every right to answer the charges leveled against a school corporation or its teaching materials.

- Teachers, librarians, administrators, and school board members have every right to point out distortions or misrepresentations of material labeled "objectionable."

- Teachers, librarians, administrators, and school board members must become familiar with the tactics and vocabulary of schoolbook protesters.

- Administrators and school board members should note the actions of the school officials in the Tell City incident. They followed their procedures; they did not panic; they did not remove books willy-nilly.

- Students should not be isolated from the controversy; rather, they can learn much by discovering how controversies can arise and how they can be resolved.

- School officials should not permit unfounded criticism to interfere with the educational process.

## 33. What steps should school systems take to prepare for censorship attempts?

1. Review the instructional materials selection policy to make certain that it is comprehensive and well written. (See question 35.)

2. Review the procedures for handling complaints about books, teaching materials, courses, and teaching methods. (See questions 36 and 37.)

3. Review the policies and procedures on handling complaints published by the American Library Association for ideas that might be incorporated into local policies and procedures.

4. Make certain that the policies and procedures adopted by the school system are readily available to all citizens.

5. Select materials that are consistent with the educational objectives of the school system and of specific classes.

6. Prepare written rationales for controversial materials. Ken Donelson, professor of English at Arizona State University, has suggested that each rationale should address these eight questions:
   a. For what classes is this book especially appropriate?
   b. To what particular objectives, literary or psychological or pedagogical, does this book lend itself?
   c. In what ways will the book be used to meet those objectives?
   d. What problems of style, tone, or theme, or possible grounds for censorship exist in the book?
   e. How does the teacher plan to meet those problems?
   f. Assuming that the objectives are met, how would students be different because of their reading of this book?
   g. What are some other appropriate books an individual student might read in place of this book?
   h. What reputable sources have recommended this book? What have critics said of it?

7. Make provisions for alternate assignments in those classes in which such assignments are feasible; for example, an English class in which novels are studied.

8. Form a support group of persons in the community who are committed to a sound education for all students.

## 34. What are the ingredients of a good materials selection policy?

The Michigan Association for Media in Education included these components of a materials selection policy in its 1977 publication, *Selection Policies: A Guide to Updating and Writing.*

### Preliminary Consideration

The committee drafting the Instructional Materials Selection Policy should *consider* including members of the following groups in order to enlist wide support for the policy: students, teachers, media specialists, parents, para-professionals, building administrators, system administrators, Regional Educational Materials Center staff (REMC).

A decision should be made at the outset as to whether the policy will cover *all* instructional materials or only those purchased by and housed in the media center.

A local level statement of Instructional Materials Selection Policy should include (not necessarily in the following order):

1. A statement of the philosophy of materials selection such as is given in the Library Bill of Rights.
2. A statement that the governing body of the district is legally responsible for the selection of instructional materials.
3. A statement detailing the delegation of this responsibility to professional personnel.
4. Criteria for instructional materials selection in the school or district.
5. Procedures for implementing selection criteria.
6. A routine procedure for challenged materials including:
   a. a complaint committee and its make-up;

   b. a statement that the procedure is applicable to *all* individuals, including school personnel *and* board members;
   c. a statement of how challenged materials will be handled during the period of reconsideration;
   d. a statement of whether or not materials will be put through the entire reconsideration process more than once within a specified time period.
7. Definitions of critical terms used in the selection policy, for example, "selection," "instructional materials," "literary merit," etc.

## 35. Are there model instructional materials selection policies that school systems can use as guides?

The instructional materials selection policies prepared by the Iowa Department of Public Instruction and by the Madison (Wisconsin) Metropolitan School District have been used widely as models. The first model policy statement below is from *Selection of Instructional Materials* (Iowa Department of Public Instruction 1977; *see* Code of Iowa 279.8, ch. 301).

### Model Statement of Policy

The Board of Directors of the _____ School District hereby declares it the policy of the District to provide a wide range of instructional materials on all levels of difficulty, with diversity of appeal, and the presentation of different points of view and to allow review of allegedly inappropriate instructional materials.

### Model Statement of Rules

I. Responsibility for Selection of Materials

   A. The Board of Directors is legally responsible for all matters relating to the operation of the _____ School District.

B. The responsibility for the selection of instructional materials is delegated to the professionally trained and certificated staff employed by the school system. For the purposes of this rule the term "instructional materials" includes printed and audiovisual materials (not equipment), whether considered text materials or media center materials.

C. While selection of materials involves many people (principals, teachers, students, supervisors, community persons and media specialists), the responsibility for coordinating the selection of most instructional materials and making the recommendation for purchase rests with certificated media personnel. For the purpose of this rule the term "media specialist" includes librarians, school media specialists or other appropriately certificated persons responsible for selection of media.

D. Responsibility for coordinating the selection of text materials for distribution to classes will rest with the appropriate department chairperson or with the Textbook Evaluation Committee. For the purpose of this rule the term "text materials" includes textbooks and other print and nonprint materials provided in multiple copies for use of a total class or a major segment of such a class.

II. Criteria for Selection of Materials

A. The following criteria will be used as they apply:
1. Materials shall support and be consistent with the general educational goals of the district and the objectives of specific courses.
2. Materials shall meet high standards of quality in factual content and presentation.
3. Materials shall be appropriate for the subject area and for the age, emotional development, ability level, and social development of the students for whom the materials are selected.
4. Materials shall have aesthetic, literary, or social value.
5. Materials chosen shall be by competent and qualified authors and producers.

6. Materials shall be chosen to foster respect for minority groups, women, and ethnic groups and shall realistically represent our pluralistic society, along with the roles and life styles open to both men and women in today's world. Materials shall be designed to help students gain an awareness and understanding of the many important contributions made to our civilization by minority groups, ethnic groups and women.

Materials shall clarify the multiple historical and contemporary forces with their economic, political, and religious dimensions which have operated to the disadvantage or advantage of women, minority groups, and ethnic groups. These materials shall present and analyze intergroup tension and conflict objectively, placing emphasis upon resolving social and economic problems.

Materials shall be designed to motivate students and staff to examine their own attitudes and behaviors and to comprehend their own duties, responsibilities, rights and privileges as participating citizens in a pluralistic, non-sexist society.

7. Materials shall be selected for their strengths rather than rejected for their weaknesses.
8. Biased or slanted materials may be provided to meet specific curriculum objectives.
9. Physical format and appearance of materials shall be suitable for their intended use.

B. The selection of materials on controversial issues will be directed toward maintaining a balanced collection representing various views.

III. Procedure for Selection

A. Media
  1. In selecting materials for purchase for the media center, the media specialist will evaluate the existing collection and the curriculum needs and will consult reputable, professionally prepared selection aids and other appropriate sources. For the purposes of this rule the term "media" includes all materials considered part of the library

collection, plus all instructional materials housed in resource centers and classrooms (if any) which are not text materials. For the purpose of this rule, the term "media center" is the space, room or complex of rooms and spaces designated as a library, media center, instructional materials center or similar term. It may include units not contiguous to the center where facilities dictate. These units would include but not be limited to resource centers, production centers, and television studios.

2. Recommendations for purchase will be solicited from faculty and student body.

3. Gift materials shall be judged by the criteria in Section II and shall be accepted or rejected by those criteria.

4. Selection is an ongoing process which should include the removal of materials no longer appropriate and the replacement of lost and worn materials still of educational value.

5. Selections are forwarded to the office of the superintendent or his or her designee (e.g., the district media director or the business manager) through the principal or other person in charge of the attendance center for purchase throughout the year.

B. Text Material

1. Text materials committees shall be appointed at the time that text adoption areas are determined. Appropriate subject area, instructional level, and media personnel shall be included in each committee.

2. Criteria for text materials consistent with the general criteria for materials selection noted in Section II shall be developed by teacher committees.

3. The committee shall present its recommendation(s) to the superintendent or other designated administrator.

4. The superintendent or his or her designee and the text materials committee shall present the recommendation(s) to the board.

IV. Objection:

A. Any resident of the school district may raise objection to instructional materials used in the district's educational program despite the fact that the individuals selecting such material were duly qualified to make the selection and followed the proper procedure and observed the criteria for selecting such material.

1. The school official or staff member receiving a complaint regarding instructional materials shall try to resolve the issue informally. The materials shall remain in use unless removed through the procedure in Section *IV. B. 6. e.* of this rule.

   a. The school official or staff member initially receiving a complaint shall explain to the complainant the school's selection procedure, criteria, and qualifications of those persons selecting the material.

   b. The school official or staff member initially receiving a complaint shall explain to the best of his or her ability the particular place the objected to material occupies in the educational program, its intended educational usefulness, and additional information regarding its use, or refer the complaining party to someone who can identify and explain the use of the material.

(Comment: The vast majority of complaints can be amicably disposed of in the first stages when the school officials and staff are frequently reminded of the school's procedures. A quick personal conference can often times solve the problem where a shift into a more formal procedure might inflate the problem. While the legal right to object to materials is not expressly stated, it is implied in such provisions as the right to petition the government for redress of grievances.)

2. In the event that the person making an objection to material is not satisfied with the initial explanation, the person raising the question should be referred to someone designated by the principal or person in charge of the attendance center to handle such complaints or to the media specialist for that attendance center. If, after private counseling, the complainant desires to file a formal complaint,

the person to whom the complainant has been referred will assist in filling out a Reconsideration Request Form in full.

3. The individual receiving the initial complaint shall advise the principal or person in charge of the attendance center where the challenged material is being used, of the initial contact no later than the end of the following school day, whether or not the complainant has apparently been satisfied by the initial contact. A written record of the contact shall be maintained by the principal or other person in charge of the attendance center.

4. The principal or other person in charge of each attendance center shall review the selection and objection rules with the staff at least annually. The staff shall be reminded that the right to object to materials is one granted by policies enacted by the Board of Directors and firmly entrenched in law. They shall also be reminded of ethical and practical considerations in attempting to handle resident complaints with courtesy and integrity.

B. Request for Reconsideration

1. Any resident or employee of the school district may formally challenge instructional materials used in the district's educational program on the basis of appropriateness. This procedure is for the purpose of considering the opinions of those persons in the schools and the community who are not directly involved in the selection process.

2. Each attendance center and the school district's central office will keep on hand and make available Reconsideration Request Forms. All formal objections to instructional materials must be made on this form.

3. The Reconsideration Request Form shall be signed by the complainant and filed with the Superintendent or someone so designated by the Superintendent.

4. Within five business days of the filing of the form, the Superintendent or person so designated by the Superintendent shall file the material in question with the

Reconsideration Committee for re-evaluation. The Committee shall recommend disposition to the office of the Superintendent.

5. Generally, access to challenged material shall not be restricted during the reconsideration process. However, in unusual circumstances, the material may be removed temporarily by following the provisions of Section *IV. B. 6. e.* of this rule.

6. The Reconsideration Committee

a. The Reconsideration Committee shall be made up of eleven members.

(1) One teacher designated annually by the Superintendent.

(2) One school media specialist designated annually by the Superintendent.

(3) One member of the central administrative staff designated annually by the Superintendent. (This position will normally be filled by the supervisor or person responsible for the district's media services.)

(4) Five members from the community appointed annually by the Executive Committee of the Parent-Teacher-Student Association.

(5) Three high school students, selected annually from and by the Student Advisory Committee.

(Comment: Subsections (4) and (5) represent a departure from the traditional approaches of handling challenged school materials and may well be the key to the success or failure of this model. A committee with a majority of lay members should be viewed by the community as being objective and not automatically supportive of prior professional decisions on selection. Much of the philosophy regarding the Committee structure was borrowed from the policy of the Cedar Rapids Community School District, Cedar Rapids, Iowa.

Use of the Parent-Teacher-Student Association in this model is merely illustrative. Whether the non-educators are selected from the P.T.S.A. or other groups interested in the community's schools is not important. The important thing is the establishment and maintenance of the Committee's credibility with the community through a majority of nonprofessionals. An appointed committee will generally be more objective than a voluntary committee.

The method of selecting students for the Committee will depend greatly upon the size and organization of the district. A district with several high schools may want to have one student from each on the committee while a district with one high school may want one student representative from each grade. Student selection of the representatives to this Committee is very important. Any responsible student group or groups may be used when a Student Advisory Committee does not exist in the district.)

  b. The chairperson of the Committee shall not be an employee or officer of the District. The secretary shall be an employee or officer of the District.

(Comment: It is vital to the operation of this model that a community member chair the Reconsideration Committee. Credibility is the watchword.)

  c. The Committee shall first meet each year during the third week in September at a time and place designated by the Superintendent and made known to the members of the Committee at least three school days in advance.

  d. A calendar of subsequent regular meetings for the year shall be established and a chairperson and a secretary selected at the first meeting.

(Comment: While many districts may not feel the need to hold regular, perhaps monthly meetings, it is important to establish a sense of continuity and regularity about the Committee. The notoriety and excitement caused by emergency meetings when challenges arise in a community may be the unnecessary fuel to cause an ordinary healthy situation to become distorted beyond proportion. It is wiser to cancel unnecessary meetings than to call unexpected ones. Lack of frequent challenges to school materials probably means that one or more of the following is present: (1) satisfaction with the selection process, (2) lack of community interest, (3) belief in the futility of communication with school district officials, or (4) undue influence on the selection and weeding processes.)

  e. Special meetings may be called by the Superintendent to consider temporary removal of materials in unusual circumstances. Temporary removal shall require a three-fourths vote of the Committee.

f. The calendar of regular meetings and notice of special meetings shall be made public through appropriate student publications and other communications methods.

g. The Committee shall receive all Reconsideration Request Forms from the Superintendent or person designated by the Superintendent.

h. The procedure for the first meeting following receipt of a Reconsideration Request Form is as follows:

(1) Distribute copies of written request form.

(2) Give complainant or a group spokesperson an opportunity to talk about and expand on the request form.

(3) Distribute reputable, professionally prepared reviews of the material when available.

(4) Distribute copies of challenged material as available.

i. At a subsequent meeting, interested persons, including the complainant, may have the opportunity to share their views. The Committee may request that individuals with special knowledge be present to give information to the committee.

j. The complainant shall be kept informed by the Secretary concerning the status of his or her complaint throughout the Committee reconsideration process. The complainant and known interested parties shall be given appropriate notice of such meetings.

k. At the second or a subsequent meeting, as desired, the Committee shall make its decision in either open or closed session. The Committee's final decision will be, (1) to take no removal action, (2) to remove all or part of the challenged material from the total school environment, or (3) to limit the educational use of the challenged material. The sole criteria for the final decision is the appropriateness of the material for its intended educational use. The vote on the decision shall be by secret ballot. The written decision and its justification shall be forwarded to the Superintendent for appropriate action, the complainant and the appropriate attendance centers.

(Comment: The state open meeting law should be reviewed for its application to this provision.)

l. A decision to sustain a challenge shall not be interpreted as a judgment of irresponsibility on the part of the professionals involved in the original selection or use of the material.

m. Requests to reconsider materials which have previously been before the Committee must receive approval of a majority of the Committee members before the materials will again be reconsidered. Every Reconsideration Request Form shall be acted upon by the Committee.

n. In the event of a severe overload of challenges, the Committee may appoint a subcommittee of members or nonmembers to consolidate challenges and to make recommendations to the full Committee. The composition of this subcommittee shall approximate the representation on the full Committee.

o. Committee members directly associated with the selection, use, or challenge of the challenged material shall be excused from the Committee during the deliberation on such materials. The Superintendent may appoint a temporary replacement for the excused Committee member, but such replacement shall be of the same general qualifications of that person excused.

(Comment: The Committee should never be placed in the position of appearing to defend itself, its members, or the school staff. The Committee must maintain a nonadversarial position.)

p. If the complainant is not satisfied with the decision, he or she may request that the matter be placed on the agenda of the next regularly scheduled meeting of the Board.

(Comment: These requests should comply with existing board policy and rules regarding the board agenda.)

q. Any person dissatisfied with the decision of the Board may appeal to the State Board of Public Instruction pursuant to state law.

(Comment: Subsections *p.* and *q.* are implicit and expressly provided for respectively, in Iowa law. Some persons might feel that it would be more appropriate to not use *p.* and *q.* as they may encourage appeals. The provisions of *q.* would not be applicable to decisions of A.E.A. Boards, but would be applicable to decisions of Area Community Technical College Boards and School District Boards.)

The following policy statement was prepared by the Madison (Wisconsin) Metropolitan School District and adopted by the district's board of education on 13 September 1982.

## Instructional Materials Selection
## Policy and Procedures

### Selection Responsibility

Pursuant to Wisconsin Statutes, the legal responsibility for the selection of instructional materials rests with the Board of Education. The purpose of this selection policy is to define the philosophy, objectives, criteria, and procedures to be followed by those groups that function as agents of the Board of Education for acquiring print and audiovisual materials for instructional programs. These groups include: Program Materials Selection (PMS) committees; Instructional Materials Center (IMC) committees; Middle and High School Paperback committees; Specialized Educational Services (SES) committees; Chapter I (Title I) materials selection committees; and *ad hoc* committees assigned to select materials for unique school programs.

Instructional materials include print and nonprint items such as audiotapes and audiocassettes, books, computer programs, dioramas, disc recordings, films, filmstrips, games, graphic works, manuscripts, maps and globes, microforms, models, multimedia kits, newspapers, overhead transparencies, pamphlets, periodicals, realia, reference materials, slides, television programs, videocassettes, videodiscs, videotapes, and various combinations of these.

### Selection Philosophy

The right to a free choice among alternatives is basic to a democratic society. It is through the exercise of the freedoms set forth in the Bill of Rights that an informed choice can take place. If there is to be freedom of speech, of the press, and of assembly, then there must also be freedom to hear, to view, to read, and to discuss. Our educational system must, therefore, allow a free access to a full range of instructional materials to insure the realization of these freedoms.

**Selection Objectives**

The basic objective of materials selection is to provide students and faculty with learning resources that are intrinsic to the implementation of curriculum and that have value for diversified interests, abilities, and maturity levels. Selected materials should:

1. stimulate thinking, provide facts, and contribute to student growth in literary and aesthetic appreciation;
2. contain ideas and information that enable students to make judgments and decisions relating to their daily lives;
3. present a diversity of viewpoints on controversial issues;
4. include the thinking and contribution of the many cultural, ethnic, and religious groups which constitute society in the United States;
5. portray a variety of lifestyles with which students can identify;
6. represent the variety of communication formats to provide for individual learning styles and to provide students the opportunity to analyze various media formats critically;
7. encourage students to read, view, and listen for pleasure and recreation, fostering a life-long appreciation of such activities.

**Selection Criteria**

Instructional materials shall support and be consistent with the general educational goals of the district. All materials should be selected on the basis of an identified need for the materials and the general suitability of the materials to the needs and abilities of those who will use them. In potentially sensitive areas (e.g., race, sex, religion, political theory and ideology), materials should be selected for their strengths and/or significance rather than rejected for their weaknesses. Consideration of the criteria below, where relevant, shall provide the basis for selection of instructional materials. The criteria are not arranged in any particular order of importance.

1. *Relation to Curriculum.*

   Materials should be selected for their contribution to the implementation of the school's curriculum.

2. *Relation to Existing Collection.*

   The materials should make a contribution to the balance of the individual school collection of materials for which they are selected.

3. *Interest and Appeal.*

   The content and style of the materials should appeal to the interests of those who will use them.

4. *Accuracy and Authenticity.*

   The content of materials should be valid, reliable, and complete. Imaginative materials should encourage worthwhile appreciations, attitudes, understandings, and insights.

5. *Authority.*

   Consideration should be given to the qualifications, reputation, and significance of those responsible for creating the material (the author, producer, publisher).

6. *Comprehension.*

   The material should be clearly presented in a well-organized fashion. The nature of concepts being developed should be appropriate both to the intended users and the depth of coverage. In print materials, the readability should correspond to the reading ability of the intended users; in nonprint materials, audiovisual representations should correspond to the comprehension level of the intended users. The materials should catch and hold the user's interest and stimulate further learning.

7. *Permanence and Timeliness.*

   The material should be of lasting value and/or should be of widespread current interest or concern.

8. *Cultural Pluralism.*

   Wisconsin Statutes (Chapter 89, Section J) mandate that students have access "to a current, well-balanced collection of books, basic reference materials, periodicals, and audiovisual materials which depict in an accurate and unbiased way the cultural diversity and pluralistic nature of American Society.''

Materials should foster respect for, and help students gain an awareness of, the many contributions made by the various groups which make up our pluralistic society. The materials should present inter-group tension and conflict objectively, placing emphasis on resolving social and economic problems.

9. *Whole vs. Part.*

Each item should be approached from a broad perspective, looking at the work as a whole and judging controversial elements in context rather than as isolated parts. Periodicals, for example, should be selected and purchased for their overall reputation, and should not be rejected because of an occasional article which may be offensive.

10. *Recency.*

In certain subject areas (science and technology, for example), materials should be examined carefully for the currency of the information presented. Copyright date should be used as one indicator of the currency of the material.

11. *Format.*

The medium selected to present the material should be appropriate to the content. For example, a series of still photographs of works of art might appropriately be presented in a filmstrip, slide program, or book rather than in a film or video tape. However, these latter media are appropriate when it is important to show motion or present a dramatization.

12. *Quality of Writing/Production.*

The material should be acceptable mechanically and artistically with each element combining to form an aesthetically pleasing whole. The material should stimulate growth in factual knowledge and/or literary appreciation. The content should provide adequate scope, range, depth, and continuity while maintaining user interest.

13. *Technical and Physical Qualities.*

Print material should be attractively presented with suitable illustrations and graphics. The size and style of type should be appropriate to the intended age level. Audio material should use sound creatively and be clear and free of distortion. The narrator should have a pleasant voice and speak with expression. Visual materials should have good picture quality and be authentic in regard to detail, color, depth, dimension, and size proportions. Original art work should be reproduced faithfully. There should be sufficient durability to meet the demands of the intended user.

14. *Cost.*

The selection of any piece of material, particularly an expensive one, should be seen in relation to the degree of need for the material, the amount of anticipated use, and existing budgetary limitations. The possibility of shared use of materials should be considered. In the event that materials are perceived to be of comparable quality, the materials of least cost shall be purchased.

15. *Treatment of Controversial Issues.*

Materials on controversial issues should be selected to represent the fullest possible range of contrasting points of view, to provide a balanced collection of materials on such subjects.

16. *Treatment of Religion.*

Materials about religion should be chosen to explain, not to indoctrinate.

17. *Treatment of Profanity, Sex, and Violence.*

The use of profanity, sexual incidents, or violence in a literary work should not automatically disqualify such material. The decision should be made on the basis of the work's general literary value, rather than on some isolated parts, and on whether it deals with situations realistically, presenting life in its true proportions.

18. *Treatment of Human Development.*

Materials on human physiology, physical maturation, or personal hygiene should be accurate and objectively presented.

19. *Treatment of Biased Materials.*

Materials which unfairly, inaccurately, or viciously treat a particular race, sex, ethnic group, age group, religion, etc., shall not be selected unless there exists a legitimate educational purpose — such as analysis, observation, historical development of interpretation — for the use of such materials. When necessary, the Department of Human Relations should be consulted in evaluating such items.

20. *Gift and Sponsored Materials.*

Gift materials and sponsored materials must meet the same criteria as those selected for purchase. They are accepted with the understanding that, if not suitable, they may be disposed of at the discretion of the school staff members who have received the materials.

Board of Education policy #3660 requires that instructional materials that carry advertising be screened and approved by a committee appointed by the Assistant Superintendent.

**Policy**

*Reconsideration of Selected Materials*

A complaint about a book or other instructional material by a resident of the Madison Metropolitan School District should be given consideration by district administrators and the Board of Education only after attempts to resolve it at the local school level have been exhausted. The use of materials being reconsidered shall not be restricted until a final deposition of the complaint has been reached. Reconsideration decisions made at one school shall not be binding on other schools.

**Procedure**

*Reconsideration of Selected Materials*

1.  Upon receipt of a complaint about a book or other instructional material, the Building Principal shall contact the complainant and appropriate school staff to discuss the complaint and attempt to resolve it by explaining the philosophy and goals of the instructional program and the selection policy and procedure.

2.  A standard questionnaire (Request for Reconsideration of Instructional Materials) and cover letter shall be sent to the complainant with a request that he/she return the completed

questionnaire to the Building Principal. The Principal shall send a duplicate of the completed questionnaire to the appropriate school staff and District Director.

3. Upon receipt of the completed questionnaire, the Principal shall appoint and convene an advisory committee consisting of appropriate school staff (including school media specialists when IMC materials are involved) and parents to consider the complaint. The committee will use the stated selection criteria in its reconsideration of a book or other instructional material, and will respond in writing to the complainant, with a copy sent to the District Director and appropriate program coordinators.

4. Following consideration by the Principal and committee, if it is the desire of the complainant, the complaint is submitted to the Superintendent for consideration.

5. Following consideration by the Superintendent, if it is the desire of the complainant, the complaint is submitted to the Board of Education.

6. The Board of Education, through the Superintendent, shall be informed of any decision at any level to remove an item from classroom or IMC use if it is the result of a complaint handled through this process.

7. Complaints submitted directly to the Superintendent and/or Board of Education shall be referred to the appropriate Building Principal.

## 36. What steps should a school system follow if a person complains about a book or some other teaching material or teaching method?

1. The person responsible for the challenged material (teacher or librarian) should be given the opportunity to meet informally with the person making the complaint. Teachers and librarians throughout the nation have reported that such meetings frequently resolve the prob-

lem. The complainant may be seeking information about how and why the book — or whatever — is used. Courteous, clear answers to the how and why frequently satisfy the complainants.

2. If a school administrator or school board member is the first to hear the complaint, he or she should not take unilateral action. Rather, the school official should take step one above (see question 39).

3. If the complainant is not satisfied as a result of the informal meeting, then he or she should be given a request for reconsideration form (see question 37).

4. On receipt of the signed request for reconsideration form, the school official handling the complaint should give the challenged material to the reconsideration committee, which should have been appointed annually (see question 35).

5. Access to the challenged material should not be limited during the period of reconsideration.

6. The decision of the reconsideration committee should be given to the superintendent. (For a more complete discussion of the steps and for a consideration of various conflicts that might arise in the reconsideration process, see the Iowa policy in question 35.)

Several school officials have told me that they believe a public hearing conducted by the reconsideration committee before it makes its decision can be valuable. Such a hearing gives various segments of the community an opportunity to speak out. The danger of such a hearing is obvious: one side may try to monopolize the meeting. But the school officials who have talked with me indicate that giving the community an opportunity to speak is well worth the risk.

## 37. What is a request for reconsideration form and when should it be used?

The following request for reconsideration form is reprinted with the permission of the American Association of School Librarians, 50 East Huron St., Chicago, IL 60611.

### REQUEST FOR RECONSIDERATION
### OF INSTRUCTIONAL MATERIALS

School _____

Please check type of material:
( ) Book          ( ) Film          ( ) Record
( ) Periodical    ( ) Filmstrip     ( ) Kit
( ) Pamphlet      ( ) Cassette      ( ) Other

Title_____
Author _____
Publisher or Producer _____
Request Initiated by _____
Telephone _____ Address _____
City _____ State _____ Zip _____

The following questions are to be answered after the complainant has read, viewed, or listened to the school library material in its entirety. If sufficient space is not provided, attach additional sheets. (Please sign your name to each additional attachment.)

1. To what in the material do you object? (Please be specific, cite pages, frames in a filmstrip, film sequence, et cetera.)

2. What do you believe is the theme or purpose of this material?

3. What do you feel might be the result of a student using this material?

4. For what age group would you recommend this material?

5. Is there anything good in this material? Please comment.

6. Would you care to recommend other school library material of the same subject and format?

_____     _____
       Signature of Complainant                 Date

Please return completed form to the school principal.

This form should be used only after the informal meeting (see question 36) if the complainant is not satisfied with the discussion and wants to take formal action to challenge the book, other teaching material, course, or teaching method.

## 38. What steps can be taken to enhance academic freedom for teachers?

Teachers in some communities have succeeded in having a clause on academic freedom included in the master contract. Here is one sample from Article XVII of the master contract of the teachers in the Fort Wayne (Indiana) School Corporation:

### Academic Freedom

It is mutually recognized that freedom carries with it responsibility; academic freedom also carries with it academic responsibility which is determined by the basic ideals, goals, and institutions of the local community. Discussion and analysis of controversial issues should be conducted within the framework of the fundamental values of the community as they are expressed in the educational philosophy and objectives of the Board.

Within the preceding frame of reference and as it pertains to the course to which a teacher is assigned, academic freedom in the Fort Wayne Community Schools is defined as:

1. The right to teach and learn about controversial issues which have economic, political, scientific, or social significance.

2. The right to use materials which are relevant to the levels of ability and maturity of the students and to the purposes of the school system.
3. The right to maintain a classroom environment which is conducive to the free exchange and examination of ideas which have economic, political, scientific or social significance.
4. The right of teachers to participate fully in the public affairs of the community.
5. The right of students to hold divergent ideas as long as the expression of their dissent is done within the guidelines of debate and discussion which are generally accepted by teachers in a normal classroom environment.
6. The right of teachers to a free expression of conscience as private citizens with the correlative responsibility of a professional presentation of balanced views relating to controversial issues as they are studied in the classroom.

The State of Connecticut took a major step toward ensuring academic freedom when it adopted its policy on academic freedom. The following is taken from the State of Connecticut Controversial Issues Policy (1981):

### Free to Learn
### A Policy on Academic Freedom and Public Education

Academic freedom is the freedom to teach and to learn. In defending the freedom to teach and to learn, we affirm the democratic process itself. American public education is the source of much that is essential to our democratic heritage. No other single institution has so significantly sustained our national diversity, nor helped voice our shared hopes for an open and tolerant society. Academic freedom is among the strengths of American public education. Attempts to deny the freedom to teach and to learn are, therefore, incompatible with the goals of excellence and equity in the life of our public schools.

With freedom comes responsibility. With rights come obligations. Accordingly, academic freedom in our public schools is subject to certain limitations. Therefore, the STATE BOARD OF EDUCATION affirms that:

115

Academic freedom in our public schools is properly defined within the context of law and the constraints of mutual respect among individuals. Public schools represent a public trust. They exist to prepare our children to become partners in a society of self-governing citizens. Therefore, access to ideas and opportunities to consider the broad range of questions and experiences which constitute the proper preparation for a life of responsible citizenship must not be defined by the interests of any single viewpoint. Teachers, school administrators, librarians, and school media specialists must be free to select instructional and research materials appropriate to the maturity level of their students. This freedom is itself subject to the reasonable restrictions mandated by law to school officials and administrators. At the same time, local school officials must demonstrate substantial or legitimate public interest in order to justify censorship or other proposed restrictions upon teaching and learning. Similarly, local boards of education cannot establish criteria for the selection of library books based solely on the personal, social or political beliefs of school board members. While students must be free to voice their opinions in the context of a free inquiry after truth and respect for their fellow students and school personnel, student expression which threatens to interfere substantially with the school's function is not warranted by academic freedom. Students must be mindful that their rights are neither absolute nor unlimited. Part of responsible citizenship is coming to accept the consequences of the freedoms to which one is entitled by law and tradition. Similarly, parents have the right to affect their own children's education, but this right must be balanced against the right other parents' children have to a suitable range of educational experiences. Throughout, the tenets of academic freedom seek to encourage a spirit of reasoned community participation in the life and practices of our public schools.

Since teaching and learning are among the missions of our public schools, the STATE BOARD OF EDUCATION affirms the distinction between teaching and indoctrination. Schools should teach students how to think, not what to think. To study an idea is not necessarily to endorse an idea. Public school classrooms are forums for inquiry, not arenas for the promulgation of particular viewpoints. While communities have the right to exercise supervision over their own public school practices and programs, their participation in the educational life of their schools should respect the constitutional and intellectual rights guaranteed school personnel and students by American law and tradition.

Accordingly, the STATE BOARD OF EDUCATION, in order to encourage improved educational practices, recommends that local school boards adopt policies and procedures to receive, review, and take action upon requests that question public school practices and programs. Community members should be encouraged, and made aware of their rights to voice their opinions about school practices and programs in an appropriate administrative forum. The STATE BOARD OF EDUCATION further recommends that local school boards take steps to encourage informed community participation in the shared work of sustaining and improving our public schools.

Finally, the STATE BOARD OF EDUCATION affirms that community members and school personnel should acknowledge together that the purpose of public education is the pursuit of knowledge and the preparation of our children for responsible citizenship in a society that respects differences and shared freedom.

## 39. What is the role of an administrator in a censorship incident?

First, the administrator should attempt to schedule an informal meeting with the complainant(s) and the person (teacher or librarian) responsible for the challenged material. Second, the administrator should refrain from taking the side of the complainant immediately, as has been the case in a number of censorship incidents throughout the nation. Unfortunately, some school administrators have commented negatively on a book without having read it. Third, the administrator should follow the procedures for handling complaints and should not remove a book unilaterally. Such action might prove embarrassing and might result in a lawsuit.

## 40. What books should teachers, librarians, and administrators read to understand the schoolbook protest movement and to be prepared to cope with it?

Joseph E. Bryson and Elizabeth W. Detty. *Censorship of Public School Library and Instructional Material.* Charlottesville, Va.: Michie Company, 1982.

Lee Burress and Edward Jenkinson. *The Student's Right to Know.* Champaign, Ill.: National Council of Teachers of English, 1983.

James E. David, ed. *Dealing with Censorship.* Champaign, Ill.: National Council of Teachers of English, 1979.

Homer Duncan. *Secular Humanism: The Most Dangerous Religion in America.* Lubbock, Tex.: Missionary Crusader, 1979.

Stanley Elam, ed. *Public Schools and the First Amendment.* Bloomington, Ind.: Phi Delta Kappa, 1983.

James C. Hefley. *Textbooks on Trial.* Wheaton, Ill.: Victor Books, 1976. (Published in paperback as *Are Textbooks Harming Your Children?* Milford, Mich.: Mott Media, 1979.)

Edward B. Jenkinson. *Censors in the Classroom.* Carbondale, Ill.: Southern Illinois University Press, 1979.

Paul Kurtz. *In Defense of Secular Humanism.* Buffalo: Prometheus Books, 1983.

Tim LaHaye. *The Battle for the Public Schools.* Old Tappan, N.J.: Fleming Revell, 1983.

Corliss Lamont. *The Philosophy of Humanism,* 4th ed., rev. New York: Philosophical Library, 1957.

Connaught Coyne Marshner. *Blackboard Tyranny.* New Rochelle, N.Y.: Arlington House, 1978.

Barbara M. Morris. *Change Agents in the Schools.* Upland, Calif.: The Barbara M. Morris Report, 1979.

Robert M. O'Neil. *Classrooms in the Crossfire: The Rights and Interests of Students, Parents, Teachers, Administrators, Librarians, and the Community.* Bloomington: Indiana University Press, 1981.

Barbara Parker and Stefanie Weiss. *Protecting the Freedom to Learn: A Citizen's Guide.* Washington, D.C.: People for the American Way, 1983.

Francis A. Schaeffer. *How Should We Then Live?* Old Tappan, N.J.: Fleming Revell, 1976.

Phyllis Schlafly. *Child Abuse in the Classroom.* Westchester, Ill.: Crossway Books, 1984.

# Footnotes

## Question 2

1. Jack Nelson and Gene Roberts, Jr., *The Censors and the Schools* (Boston: Little, Brown and Company, 1963), pp. 24-26.
2. Ibid., p. 26.
3. Ibid., pp. 24-33.
4. Reported in Edward B. Jenkinson, *Censors in the Classroom* (Carbondale: Southern Illinois University Press, 1979), p. 37.
5. Several monographs and articles referred to the Kanawha County incident as "The Battle of the Books." See, for example, footnotes 6 and 8 below.
6. The summary of the Kanawha County textbook battle is based on Franklin Parker's fastback *The Battle of the Books: Kanawha County* (Bloomington, Ind.: Phi Delta Kappa Educational Foundation, 1975); and on *Kanawha County West Virginia: A Textbook Study in Cultural Conflict* (Washington, D.C.: National Education Association, n.d.).
7. James C. Hefley, *Textbooks on Trial* (Wheaton, Ill.: Victor Books, 1976), p. 166.
8. John Egerton, "The Battle of the Books," *The Progressive* (June 1975): p. 13.

## Question 3

1. "Survey Reports Rise in School Library Censorship," *Newsletter on Intellectual Freedom*, January 1983, p. 1. Also based on comments made to the author by Lee Burress in correspondence, telephone calls, and conversations.
2. Ibid.
3. *Indianapolis Star*, 31 December 1978, p. 1. *Los Angeles Times*, 3 June 1978, p. 1.
4. Speech at a University of Minnesota Conference, 26 January 1983.
5. *Limiting What Students Shall Read: Books and Other Learning Materials in Our Public Schools: How They Are Selected and How They Are Removed*, Sponsored by the Association of American Publishers, the American Library Association, and the Association for Supervision and Curriculum Development, 1981, p. 3.
6. Mimeographed memorandum to Members of the Oregon Educational Media Association from the Intellectual Freedom Committee, 28 February 1984, p. 2.

7. Shirley Fitzgibbons, Judith Allen, Rachel Brown, and Catherine Howard, "Selection and Censorship in Indiana School Libraries: Summary Report on the Intellectual Freedom Survey," *Indiana Media Journal* (Winter 1983): 26.

8. Duplicated copy of an article by Amy McClure titled "Censorship in Ohio: It *IS* Happening Here," sent to the author by Professor McClure on 22 September 1982.

9. *Attacks on the Freedom to Learn: Lessons of Fear (1982-83)* and *Attacks on the Freedom to Learn: A 1983-84 Report*, published by People for the American Way, Washington, D.C.

## Question 4
1. *Donahue*, 17 January 1978 and 20 February 1980.
2. Statement made by Mel Gabler on *Donahue*, 17 January 1978.

## Question 6
1. Interview on *The MacNeil-Lehrer Report*, 20 February 1982.
2. Reported in the *Newsletter on Intellectual Freedom*, January 1983, p. 26.
3. Reported in the *Newsletter on Intellectual Freedom*, May 1980, p. 53.

## Question 7
1. Lester Asheim, "Not Censorship but Selection," *Wilson Library Bulletin* (September 1952): 67.
2. Doctor from Kenosha, Wisconsin, on *Donahue*, 17 January 1978.
3. Max Rafferty, "Should Schoolmen Serve as Censors?" *The Nation's Schools* (September 1964): 62. Quoted by June Edwards in "Do We Censor or Select — The Perennial Question," *Arizona English Bulletin* 22, No. 1 (1979).
4. Julia T. Bradley, "Censoring the School Library: Do Students Have the Right to Read?" *Connecticut Law Review* 10 (Spring 1978): 770.
5. "How Fair Are Your Children's Textbooks" (Washington, D.C.: National Education Association, n.d.).

## Question 9
1. Tinker v. Des Moines Independent Commun. School District, 393 U.S. 503 (1969).
2. Tinker, p. 506.

## Question 10
1. Alan Levine, *The Rights of Students* (New York: E.P. Dutton, 1973), p. 19.
2. Ibid.

3. Pierce v. Society of Sisters, 268 U.S. 510 (1924).

4. Wisconsin v. Yoder, 406 U.S. 205 (1972).

5. Tinker v. Des Moines Independent Commun. School District, 393 U.S. 503 (1969).

6. Julia T. Bradley, "Censoring the School Library: Do Students Have the Right to Read?" *Connecticut Law Review* (Spring 1978): 760.

7. Ibid., p. 761.

8. Ibid., p. 750.

**Question 11**

1. Mailloux v. Kiley, 448 F.2d 1242 (1st Cir. 1971).

2. Ibid.

3. Ibid.

4. Stephen R. Goldstein, "The Asserted Constitutional Right of Public School Teachers to Determine What They Teach," *University of Pennsylvania Law Review* 124 (June 1976): 1324.

5. Ibid., p. 1356.

6. Cary v. Board of Educ. of the Adams-Arapahoe School Dist. 28-J, Aurora, Colorado, 427 F.Supp. 945-952 (D. Colo. 1977).

7. Ibid., p. 950.

8. Keefe v. Geanakos, 418 F.2d 359 (1st Cir. 1969).

9. Wiemann v. Updegraff, 344 U.S. 183 (1952).

10. Parducci v. Rutland, 316 F.Supp. 352 (M.D. Ala. 1970).

11. Ibid., pp. 353-354.

12. Ibid., pp. 355-356.

13. Ibid., p. 356.

14. Martha M. McCarthy and Nelda H. Cambron, *Public School Law: Teachers' and Students' Rights* (Boston: Allyn and Bacon, 1981): 49.

15. Ibid.

16. State ex rel. Wailewski v. Board of School Directors, 14 Wis. 2d 243, 111 N.W.2d 198 (1961).

17. Ahern v. Board of Education, 327 F.Supp. 1391 (D. Neb. 1971), *aff'd*, 456 F.2d 399 (8th Cir. 1972).

18. Birdwell v. Hazel School District, 352 F.Supp. 613 (E.D. Mo. 1972), *aff'd*, 491 F.2d 490 (8th Cir. 1974).

19. Adams v. Campbell County School District, 511 F.2d 1242 (10th Cir. 1975).

**Question 12**

1. Robert M. O'Neil, "Libraries, Liberty and the First Amendment," *University of Cincinnati Law Review* 42, no. 2 (1973): 209.

2. President's Council, Dist. 25 v. Community School Bd. No. 25, 457 F.2d 292 (2d Cir. 1972).
3. 409 U.S. 999-1000 (1972).
4. O'Neil, p. 212.
5. Ibid., p. 252.
6. Julia T. Bradley, "Censoring the School Library: Do Students Have the Right to Read?" *Connecticut Law Review* (Spring 1978): 757-58.
7. News release prepared by the United Teachers of Island Trees, 7 October 1976, p. 1.
8. Ibid., p. 2.
9. Ibid.
10. Brief of American Jewish Committee, et al., submitted in the United States District Court for the Eastern District of New York in the case of *Pico* v. *Board of Education, Island Trees Union Free School District*, p. 7.
11. Pico v. Island Trees School District, 474 F.Supp. 387 (E.D. N.Y. 1979).
12. R. Bruce Rich, "The Supreme Court's Decision in *Island Trees*," *Newsletter on Intellectual Freedom*, September 1982, p. 149.
13. Ibid, pp. 174-75.
14. Minarcini v. Strongsville City School District, 384 F.Supp. 698 (1974), *aff'd*, 541 F.2d 577 (6th Cir. 1976).
15. Right to Read Defense Committee of Chelsea v. School Committee of the City of Chelsea, 454 F.Supp. 703 (D. Mass. 1978).
16. Salvail v. Nashua Bd. of Education, 469 F.Supp. 1269 (D.N.H. 1979).
17. Bicknell v. Vergennes Union High School Bd. of Directors, 638 F.2d 438 (2d Cir. 1980).
18. Zykan v. Warsaw Commun. School Corp., 631 F.2d 1300 (7th Cir. 1980).
19. Pratt v. Independent School Dist. No. 831, 670 F.2d 771 (8th Cir. 1982).

## Question 13

1. David Schimmel and Louis Fisher, *The Rights of Parents in the Education of Their Children* (Columbia, Md.: National Committee for Citizens in Education, 1977), p. 82.
2. Ibid., p. 89.
3. Robert O'Neil, *Classrooms in the Crossfire* (Bloomington: Indiana University Press, 1981), p. 58.
4. Ibid., p. 56.

## Question 16

1. Ken Donelson, "Censorship: Some Issues and Problems," *Theory into Practice* (June 1975): 193.

**Question 17**

1. *Organizing an Effective Parent Group: Action Kit #1* (Washington, D.C.: American Education Coalition, n.d.), pp. 4-5. Although no date is given for the publication, the group was formed in 1984.
2. Ibid., pp. 6-7.
3. Ibid., pp. 8-11.
4. Ibid., pp. 21-22.
5. Ibid., pp. 22-23.
6. Ibid., pp. 26-30.
7. Ibid., pp. 31-32.
8. Connaught Coyne Marshner, *Blackboard Tyranny* (New Rochelle, N.Y.: Arlington House, 1978), p. 191.
9. Ibid., p. 239.
10. Ibid., p. 242.
11. Ibid., p. 246.
12. Mimeographed, undated document titled "Getting Involved in Your Area" and distributed by The MEL GABLERs, p. 2.
13. Mel and Norma Gabler, "A Parent's Guide to Textbook Review and Reform," *Education Update* (Winter 1978), Heritage Foundation, Washington, D.C.

**Question 19**

1. *The MEL GABLERs Educational Research Analysts NEWSLETTER*, May 1981, p. 1.
2. Mimeographed sheet distributed by the Gablers titled "FOR YOUR CONSIDERATION..."
3. Mimeographed sheet distributed by the Gablers.
4. Mimeographed sheet distributed by the Gablers titled "1978 Report" and mailed in November 1978. p. 2.
5. William Martin, "The Guardians Who Slumbereth Not," *Texas Monthly* (November 1982): 148.
6. Ibid.
7. "The World According to the Gablers: Ruminations from God's Angry Couple," *Texas Monthly* (November 1982): 151.
8. Bill of Particulars on the Houghton Mifflin Company's *Serendipity* submitted by the Gablers on 8 August 1974.
9. Bill of Particulars on the Goodheart-Willcox Company's *Homemaking Skills for Everyday Living* submitted by the Gablers in 1981.
10. Bill of Particulars on Ginn and Company's *Living, Learning, and Caring* submitted by the Gablers in 1981.

11. Bill of Particulars on the Globe Book Company's *Exploring American Citizenship* submitted by the Gablers in 1981.
12. "TEXTBOOK REVIEWING BY CATEGORIES," a mimeographed, undated outline distributed by the Gablers.

## Question 20

1. *Education Week*, 25 January 1984, p. 17.
2. *New York Times*, 15 August 1982, p. 1.
3. *Education Week*, op. cit.
4. Reported in Edward B. Jenkinson, *Censors in the Classroom* (Carbondale, Ill.: Southern Illinois University Press, 1979), p. 77.
5. *Fort Worth Star-Telegram*, 27 October 1982, p. 10A.
6. Mimeographed sheet distributed by the Gablers and titled *1978 Report* and mailed in November 1978, p. 2.
7. Letter from Professor Gerald Skoog to Joe Kelly Butler, Chairman of the Texas State Board of Education, 6 May 1983.
8. From the 1983 Texas Textbook Proclamation.
9. Reported in the *Newsletter on Intellectual Freedom*, July 1984, p. 97.
10. Testimony of Edward Jenkinson before the Texas State Board of Education, 12 May 1983.

## Question 22

1. Jerry Falwell, "Textbooks in Public Schools: A Disgrace and Concern to America," *Journal Champion*, 4 May 1979, p. 1.
2. Ibid.
3. *Spotlight*, 14 May 1979, p. 1.
4. Letter to Fellow North Carolinians from H. Lamarr Mooneyham, State Chairman, Moral Majority of North Carolina, Inc., p. 3.
5. *Raleigh News & Observer*, 1 June 1981, p. 8.
6. *Los Angeles Times News Service*, 22 March 1981.
7. *The News & The Daily Advance*, Lynchburg, Virginia, 23 November 1980, p. B-12.
8. Ibid., 23 May 1981, p. A-3.

## Question 23

1. James R. Larson, "How I Survived My Encounter with the New Right," *The Executive Editor* (January 1983): 22.

## Question 24

1. William Martin, "The Guardians Who Slumbereth Not," *Texas Monthly* (November 1982): 148.

**Question 25**

1. Tim LaHaye, *The Battle for the Mind* (Old Tappan, N.J.: Fleming Revell, 1980), p. 9.
2. LaHaye, *The Battle for the Public Schools* (Old Tappan, N.J.: Fleming Revell, 1983), p. 13.
3. Mimeographed sheet included in a packet sent to a concerned parent by Educational Research Analysts.
4. LaHaye, *The Battle for the Public Schools*, pp. 71-97.
5. Ibid., pp. 36-42, 173-202, 227-238, 71-97, 203-226.
6. Janet Egan of Parents of Minnesota, Inc., on the *MacNeil/Lehrer Report*, 20 February 1980.
7. From the Introduction to Homer Duncan's *Secular Humanism: The Most Dangerous Religion in America* (Lubbock, Tex.: Missionary Crusader, 1979), p. 4.

**Question 28**

1. This figure is based on informal summaries I have conducted in speeches to teachers and administrators in 33 states.
2. Torcaso v. Watkins, 367 U.S. 488 (1961).
3. United States v. Seeger, 380 U.S. 163 (1965).
4. *Congressional Record — Senate*, 6 June 1984, S 6674.
5. Memorandum of the American Civil Liberties Union on "The Constitutionality of Section 709 of the Education for Economic Security Act of 1984: The 'Secular Humanism' Ban," 12 April 1985, p. 1.
6. Ibid., p. 19.

**Question 29**

1. From a mimeographed transcript of the decision in *Grove* v. *Mead*, United States District Court, Eastern District of Washington.
2. From the brief filed by Michael Farris in the United States District Court, Eastern District of Tennessee.

**Question 30**

1. *Congressional Record — Senate*, 19 February 1985, S 1389.
2. Ibid.
3. Ibid.

**Question 31**

1. The summary of the Tell City schoolbook controversy is based on Edward B. Jenkinson, "The Tale of Tell City: An Anti-Censorship Saga" (a discussion paper published by People for the American Way, May 1983,

pp. 1-15); and in Edward B. Jenkinson, "The Censorship Tale of Tell City," *Indiana English* (Spring 1983): 21-28.

Sources I used to report the Tell City incident included cassette tapes of all of the proceedings of the January, February, and March meetings of the school board. Also, tapes of the Tell City book rally in February 1982, and tapes of two radio broadcasts critical of the school system. Also, letters from, and an interview with, the superintendent of schools, as well as letters to him from local citizens. Finally, clippings from area newspapers (*Tell City News, Evansville Press*, and *Louisville Courier-Journal*) for January, February, and March of 1982.